Laughter in the Dark
The Plays of Joe Orton

Arthur Burke

GE

GREENWICH EXCHANGE
LONDON

Greenwich Exchange, London

Printed and bound by Quorn Selective Repro Ltd, Loughborough
Tel: 01509 213456
Cover design, typesetting and layout by Albion Associates, London
Tel: 020 8852 4646

Greenwich Exchange Website: www.greenex.co.uk

ISBN 1-871551-56-0

CONTENTS

A note on the text

The page references for *Fred and Madge* and *The Visitors* refer to the 1998 Nick Hern Books publication of the two plays. Those for *Up Against It* refer to the 1979 Methuen publication of the screenplay. All other page references refer to the 1976 Methuen publication of *Orton – The Complete Plays*.

Acknowledgements

I should like to thank James Hodgson for setting this project in train and for his stimulating criticism of my early drafts. I should also like to thank Lisa Jenkins for her support and for allowing me to tap into her own considerable understanding of Orton and his plays. Most of all, I am grateful to my father, Dr T.E. Burke, for seventeen years of nurturing my writing with great patience, intelligence and humour.

Chronology

1933   John Kingsley Orton is born on January 1 in Leicester.

1949   Begins acting with Leicester Drama Society, Bats Players, Vaughan Players.

1951   Goes to the Royal Acadamy of Dramatic Art where he meets Kenneth Halliwell.

1953   Works as assistant stage manager at Ipswich rep.
    – Orton and Halliwell write a novel, *The Silver Bucket*.

1954 to 1956
    They write the novels *Lord Cucumber*, *The Mechanical Womb*, *The Last Days of Sodom* and *The Boy Hairdresser* (all published in 1998).

1957   Orton writes *Between Us Girls* (published 1998).

1959   Writes his first play, *Fred and Madge* (published 1998).

1961   Writes the novel, *The Vision of Gombold Proval* (published 1971 as *Head to Toe*).

1962   Writes his second play, *The Visitors* (published 1998).
    – Orton and Halliwell are arrested for stealing and damaging library books – they are sentenced to six months in prison.
    – Writes *The Ruffian on the Stair* in prison.

1963   Writes *Entertaining Mr Sloane*.

1964   *Entertaining Mr Sloane* is produced on May 6 at the New Arts Theatre Club, London.
    – Writes *The Good and Faithful Servant* and *Loot*
    – *The Ruffian on the Stair* is broadcast on 31 August by BBC Radio.

1965 *Loot* tours unsuccessfully.
– Writes *The Erpingham Camp*.
– *Entertaining Mr Sloane* opens on 12 October on Broadway.

1966 *Loot* begins a successful run in London.
– Writes *Funeral Games*.
– *The Erpingham Camp* is broadcast on 27 June by Rediffusion Television.

1967 On 11 January, *Loot* wins Evening Standard Award for Best Play of 1966.
– Writes *Up Against It*, a screenplay intended for the Beatles.
– *Crimes of Passion* (a double-bill of *The Ruffian on the Stair* and *The Erpingham Camp*) opens on 6 June at the Royal Court, London.
– Writes *What the Butler Saw*.
– On 9 August, Halliwell beats Orton to death before committing suicide.

Chapter One
A lucky man who made the grade

There is a danger that Joe Orton's life will always be more famous than his works. His biography has all the elements needed for a good story - a rags to riches tale, plenty of sex and violence, a love doomed to end in tragedy and a star-studded supporting cast. Most of all, it is the story of a talent cut off in its prime.

He was born John Kingsley Orton on 1 January 1933. He grew up in the Saffron Lane Estates of Leicester. His father, William, was a gardener for the city council. His mother, Elsie, worked as a machinist in a clothes factory until failing eyesight forced her to leave and become a cleaning woman. The Ortons were not a happy family. Joe's sister, Leonie, described her mother as 'a cruel bitch.' William was a timid man, dominated by his wife and despised by his son. Joe's first comment on hearing that his father had fractured his skull in an accident was: 'That won't make any difference to his brain.'

Early life
Elsie believed John to be the clever one of the family. This was despite his borderline illiteracy and a brogue so thick that even fellow Leicastrians had trouble understanding him. She paid for him to go to Clark's College. What she didn't realize was that Clark's was a commercial rather than an academic institution. She wanted him to receive an Eliza Doolittle education and learn how to speak fluent middle class. Clark's taught him typing and shorthand. The typing skills served him well when he became a playwright. The shorthand was useful only for recording his teenage masturbatory fantasies in a form his mother couldn't understand.

He always dreamed of the extraordinary – his favourite books were *Peter Pan, Alice in Wonderland* and the collected Greek myths – but his background pushed him towards the ordinary. A working class boy with basic secretarial skills was natural fodder for menial office jobs. He drifted from one to another. He was not happy, as his early diaries show:

> Went to bed feeling ill at the thought of work tomorrow.
> (9 January 1949)

> I wish I belonged to one of the idle rich and didn't have to work. (14 January 1949)

He could, however, indulge his fantastical tastes by taking part in amateur dramatics. He auditioned for the Leicester Dramatic Society's production of *Richard III* and was selected to play two very small parts. The chance to run onstage and shout: 'My lord, I have a message!' before an audience of the cast's relatives was enough to make him dedicate the rest of his life to the theatre. Even before his first appearance, he sat in the auditorium of the LDS's Little Theatre and dreamed of his future fame:

> Found myself thinking what I would say when asked to take part in a broadcast called *How I Became an Actor*. Probably start 'I think I have always had a sort of yearning...'
> (Diary, 3 April 1949)

> I know now I shall always want to act and I can no more sit in an office all my life than fly. (13 April 1949)

The Orton who dreamed of fame soon lost patience with the small-time dreams of the Leicester girls. While there is no evidence at this point to suggest his homosexuality, he was sure he did not want to settle down with a northern lass whose only ambition was to have a fleet of children and unfeasibly large hair.

A way out

During the run of *Richard III*, he conceived the idea of going to the Royal Academy of Dramatic Art (RADA.) He was advised to take elocution lessons to improve his chances of being accepted. The Henry

Higgins of his mother's dreams appeared in the form of a woman calling herself Madame Rothery. She had little faith in him as an actor but she smoothed out his irritable vowels and gave him the confidence to apply to RADA on 6 November 1950. He auditioned a piece from *Peter Pan* in which he leapt from one side of the stage to the other to play both Captain Hook and Smee. To the surprise of many people back home, he was accepted. Madame Rothery commented sniffily: 'It was just after the war and men were extremely scarce; so they would have taken practically anything that could stand up.'

His time at RADA was first delayed by appendicitis and then jeopardized by a call-up from the army. He had previously looked forward to joining up, seeing it as a break from the monotony of work. The army now threatened his acting career so he set out to fail the medical. As the scabs fell off his appendectomy scar, he glued them back on to make the wound look worse. He had never touched a cigarette before but started smoking several packs of unfiltered Gauloises a day in the hope of bringing on an asthma attack. At the medical itself, he had the inspiration of faking deafness in one ear. The army doctor decided that Orton was not the military type.

Kenneth Halliwell

He duly went off to RADA where he met the man who was to become the most important figure in his life: the man who made possible – and abruptly ended – his career as a playwright. Kenneth Halliwell was born on 23 June 1926 in Bebington, a suburb of Liverpool. As a child, he clung devotedly to his mother, Daisy. When he was eleven, she was stung on the tongue by a wasp. She choked to death in front of him. He never fully recovered from the loss of his mother and became quiet, moody and introspective. He and his father, Charles, had nothing to say to each other. Twelve years after his mother's death, Kenneth came downstairs to find Charles with his head in the gas oven. He had committed suicide without leaving a note.

Like Orton, Halliwell found relief from everyday tedium in the theatre. Unlike Orton, he did not have to content himself with playing small parts. He joined the Carlton Players and took a number of prominent rôles. Edna Rowson, one of the leaders of the company, described him as 'an exceptionally good actor by any standards.'

He had done well at school and his teachers had encouraged him to apply to Oxford or Cambridge to read Classics. But he had other plans for his future. He was obsessed with the idea of fame and of being hailed a great actor. He saw acting as a way of getting the attention of which he had been deprived by his mother's death. This prompted him to apply to RADA. He was accepted but did not have a happy time there. He was considerably older than the other students. He was bad tempered and pretentious. His younger, more talented colleagues feared and disliked him. His unpopularity made him increasingly sullen and introverted - not the qualities that make for good acting. His voice when performing became a strangled croak and his body was so tense that he moved round the stage like a wooden puppet. This did not stop him from talking at length about his grand schemes to revolutionize British theatre. His grandiose ambitions seemed laughably at odds with his modest talents. Nobody could take him seriously - except Orton.

Orton saw Halliwell as an educated man of the world who could teach him what books to read, what plays to see, what clothes to wear. Halliwell could give Orton the education he needed to become a writer. Halliwell saw Orton as someone who appreciated his talents and would follow him with the awestruck devotion of a pet dog. They became lovers.

After RADA, Orton and Halliwell had brief, unsuccessful stints at repertory theatres. In 1959, Halliwell bought a small flat at 25 Noel Road, Islington. He and Orton lived there until they died. At a time when homosexuality was still illegal in Britain, two gay men were taking a risk by setting up home together. There was a danger of blackmail, violence and imprisonment if the wrong person discovered that they were gay. However, the chance of discovery was not as great then as it would be now. Because it was illegal, homosexuality was less visible and less widely suspected. Today, any two men who share a flat will inevitably face rumours about their sleeping arrangements. In 1959, two bachelors could share a flat in Holmes and Watson fashion. It would not even have occurred to most people to wonder if they were sleeping together.

From stage to page

Orton and Halliwell quickly became disenchanted with acting and began to write. To begin with, Orton just typed Halliwell's words. Soon, he began to contribute his own ideas. Their novel, *The Last Days of Sodom*, interested readers at both Hamish Hamilton and Faber but was deemed too eccentric for publication. Charles Monteith at Faber wrote to them: 'I really am sorry to have to send back a manuscript which I enjoyed so much.' After this rejection, Orton and Halliwell decided to write separately. The first novel credited solely to John Orton was *Between Us Girls*. He submitted it on 2 June 1957 and it was returned to him three days later. It was finally published posthumously in October 1998. His second solo effort, *The Vision of Gombold Proval*, was also rejected by Monteith who described the book as 'several degrees too odd.' It was published as *Head to Toe* in 1971.

Orton then abandoned the novel as a literary form and began to write drama. His first play was *Fred and Madge* – a messy but entertaining fantasy about escape from working class drudgery. It was never performed in his lifetime and was not published until October 1998. He followed this with *The Visitors*. In contrast to *Fred and Madge*, this was slice of life realism. It was praised, and then rejected, by both the Royal Court and the BBC. The comment from the BBC was: 'excellent dialogue... the flaw is lack of shaping and dramatic impact'.

Depressed by failure, Orton and Halliwell found a different outlet for their anger and mischief. Orton was incensed that his local library filled its shelves with so much rubbish that there was no room for a work as important as Gibbon's *Decline and Fall of the Roman Empire*.

They took their revenge on the library in a series of imaginative defacements of the books. A gorilla's head appeared in the centre of the rose on the cover of the *Collins Guide to Roses*. Phyllis Hambledon's *Queen's Favourite* now featured two semi-naked men wrestling on its cover. In the biography of pathologist Bernard Spilsbury, above the caption 'The remains in the cellar of no. 39 Hilldrop Crescent,' a photograph showing a mound of earth and bones had been replaced with David's painting of Marat dead in his bath. At 9am on 28 April 1962, two police officers arrived to search the flat in Noel Road for stolen and defaced books. In court, Orton and Halliwell pleaded guilty to five charges of theft and malicious damage. They were sentenced to six months in prison.

For Halliwell, a prison sentence was just another example of his failure. He had failed as an actor, failed as a writer and had ended up in the place for people who have failed in life. For Orton, on the other hand, it provided a focus for his anger. Even by the standards of the day, the sentence was unduly harsh. He believed that the authorities had realised they were gay and had punished them more for their sexuality than for their crimes. As a consequence, he lost all faith in conventional morality, which he saw as a smokescreen to hide the establishment's hypocrisy and its fear of human nature. His anger with the police emerged clearly in *Loot*. His more general mistrust of authority can be seen throughout his plays.

Initial success

While in prison, Orton wrote a forty-five minute radio play, originally called *The Boy Hairdresser* but later retitled *The Ruffian on the Stair*. This was his breakthrough. In 1963, it was accepted by the BBC Third Programme. Its producer, John Tydeman, introduced Orton to Peggy Ramsay, a formidable, eccentric and much-loved theatrical agent. It was Ramsay who suggested that Orton change his name. To her ears, 'John Orton' sounded uncomfortably like 'John Osborne', the playwright who had made a huge impact on London theatre in 1956 with his *Look Back In Anger*. On 19 December 1963, Orton sent her a copy of his first full-length stage play, *Entertaining Mr Sloane*. She had reservations about it but showed it to Michael Codron, artistic director of the New Arts Theatre. He described it as 'unique stuff... totally fresh.' He and his associate Donald Albery decided very quickly that they wanted to present it.

Orton dedicated *Entertaining Mr Sloane* to Halliwell and sometimes referred to it as 'our play,' but, even at this stage in Orton's success, Halliwell began to be sidelined. Patrick Dromgoole, who directed, became furious if Halliwell tried to involve himself in the production process.

The play opened at the New Arts on 6 May 1964. The response to it was mixed. W.A. Darlington, writing for the *Daily Telegraph*, said: 'Not for a long time have I disliked a play so much as I disliked Joe Orton's *Entertaining Mr Sloane*'. For Orton, any publicity was good publicity and he wrote letters to *The Telegraph's* editor, fanning the flames of the Sloane controversy. Calling himself Peter Pinnell, he described the play as 'a highly sensationalised, lurid, crude and over-dramatised picture of life at its lowest.' As Edna Welthorpe (Mrs), he agreed with Mr Pinnell. Mrs Welthorpe declared herself 'nauseated by this endless parade of mental and physical perversion.' As Donald H. Hartley, however, he hailed the play as an 'oasis in the wasteland' of dreary theatre. His most fulsome praise of his own work was delivered under the name of Alan Crosby. Mr Crosby considered: '... a) the dialogue brilliant; b) the comedy breathtaking; c) the drama satisfying; d) the play as a whole well-written if not profound...'

One person, other than Orton in his many guises, who admired *Entertaining Mr Sloane* was Terence Rattigan, author of the highly successful plays, *French Without Tears* and *While the Sun Shines*. His comment on it was: 'To me, in some ways, it was better than Wilde because it had more bite.' Rattigan gave an important boost to Orton's career. The show had lost money at the New Arts and Albery was unsure whether he should 'bring it in' to the West End. Rattigan ensured the play's future by investing three thousand pounds in its transfer. He explained his generosity by saying: 'I don't think we're going to make any money out of this, but this talent has to be nurtured.' Rattigan had other reasons for promoting the play. He was a homosexual of the previous generation, who wrote heterosexual drama in deference to the theatrical constraints of his day. In championing *Entertaining Mr Sloane*, he was sponsoring Orton to say the things that he had not been allowed to say himself.

The play opened in the West End on 29 June 1964. It was voted joint winner (with Bill Naughton's *Alfie*) in Variety's London Critics' Poll for best new British play.

Orton's comedy is somewhat muted in *Entertaining Mr Sloane*. The play is too realistic to encompass the outrageousness of his later work. This is still more noticeable in his next play, *The Good and Faithful Servant* – a bitter, and rather depressing, television drama about an old man who realizes that he has wasted his life. It was only with *Loot* that Orton began to explore farce, a genre that allowed his characters the freedom to behave with the gleeful disregard for convention that became his trademark. *Loot* eventually became the biggest success that he lived to enjoy. The process that led to this triumph, however, was a long and painful one.

Loot

He originally set out to write a play about a nurse who murders her patients for their money. The policeman investigating her, Inspector Truscott, was to be a comparatively minor figure in her story. Then, when the play was half-written, Codron introduced Orton to Kenneth Williams, the character actor best remembered for his parts in the *Carry On* films and for the range of comic voices he provided for the radio shows *Beyond Our Ken* and *Round the Horne*. Williams was a great raconteur whose voice moved from Sloane Square to Peckham and back again in the course of a single sentence. Orton was impressed by Williams' feeling for language and manner of speaking. He became intrigued by the idea of the Williams voice speaking the Orton lines. As he left, he told Williams: 'I'm writing something at the moment. I'll write it for you.' He went home and started the second act of

Loot, beefing up the part of Truscott to make it a suitable vehicle for Williams. The result was a disjointed play in which the nurse, Fay, dominated the action in Act One but was completely overshadowed by Truscott in Act Two. Williams accepted the part but had serious doubts about the play. Just before the play opened, he wrote in his diary:

> I can't feel any sense of construction in this piece at the moment – perhaps it's the lack of any audience reaction: but this is the worst period of all, waiting to see if the thing will be able to fly... (*Kenneth Williams' Diary*, 30 January 1965)

Loot opened in Cambridge. Orton summed up the evening succinctly in a letter to Halliwell: 'The play is a disaster.' The *Cambridge Review* described it as 'an evening of very British rubbish.' The *Cambridge News* was even more damning: 'a very bad play – shapeless and without style, inexcusably vulgar and even boring.'

Orton began a long process of rewriting. The performers were set a task requiring partitions in the mind – rehearsing the rewrites in the afternoon while performing the original in the evening. They soon lost faith in the project:

> Rehearsed on the rewrites all day. In the evening the result was an unconfident performance and a gain of one laugh for the loss of another... After the show I felt so suicidally depressed I just didn't know what to do. The utter shambles of this production is totally unbelievable. The cast is demoralised and the script practically in rags and some of it complete nonsense. I wish I had never set foot near the rotten mess of it all. (*Kenneth Williams' Diary*, 10 February 1965)

Williams did what he always did when the show wasn't working. He became more and more Kenneth Williams. He knew he could usually get an audience on his side simply by living up to his public persona so he hid behind his flared-nostril mugging and stock voices. It did not work for him this time. The Williams persona was too much at odds with the Truscott character. Orton wrote to Halliwell from Oxford: 'Everyone on the verge of a nervous breakdown. Kenneth Williams disastrous - just all his old performances from *Beyond Our Ken*. And then he wonders why he isn't getting laughs. 'Ow many 'usbands 'ave you 'ad? (ugh!)...'

After the show on 16 February, Geraldine McEwan, who played Fay, came off-stage in hysterics shouting: 'I can't go on with this stuff any more! I can't go on!' She had to be taken home and sedated. Williams and McEwan asked Codron not to bring the play in to London:

> He said if the company were keen, he [Codron] could put it in the Lyric, Hammersmith. They said no. So it died tonight after 56 performances of about 3 different editions. (*Kenneth Williams' Diary*, 20 March 1965)

Exhausted by rewrites and sick of the theatre, Orton went off for the first of many holidays in Morocco with Halliwell. There he discovered hash cake and a plethora of young boys who would satisfy his every sexual whim – for a small fee. He recovered sufficiently to spend the rest of 1965 writing *The Erpingham Camp* – an extended sketch about a revolution in a British holiday camp

In January 1966, Oscar Lewenstein picked up the option on *Loot* and brought in Braham Murray, the darling of the Oxford Review, to direct. Orton presented Murray with a new version of the script. He had cut out 621 lines and the dialogue that remained was fast, funny and epigrammatical. He had also given the play unity by making Truscott the central character throughout. He had drawn on his experiences of feeling intimidated by the police to make Truscott less bumbling and more menacing. Murray's version opened in Manchester. The *Daily Telegraph* called it 'very funny' and 'as fast and furious as Feydeau'. Despite this, *Loot*'s troubled past made people reluctant to bring it in. The Royal Court expressed an interest but then decided not to put it on. On 18 June, Orton wrote to Ramsay from Morocco: 'I think you'd better warn Oscar that if the *Loot* option runs out in January with no sign of the play being put on I shan't renew the option. I shall throw the play on the fire. And I shan't write a third stage play. I shall earn my living on TV'.

Orton did not have to carry out his threat. Charles Marowitz was drafted in to direct the play at the Jeanetta Cochrane Theatre - an off West End venue at which the play could be tried on a London audience without the risk of too much capital. It opened on 27 September 1966. The *Sunday Telegraph* described it as 'the most genuinely quick-witted, pungent and sprightly entertainment by a new young British playwright for a decade.' On 1 November, it transferred to the Criterion Theatre and on 11 January 1967, it was announced winner of the *Evening Standard* award for best play of 1966. The award boosted the audiences as did the – wildly exaggerated – rumours that the film rights had been sold for £100,000.

One of the beautiful people

Things went from good to better. The day after the announcement of the award, Orton found himself courted by the cultural icons of the decade. Walter Shenson, producer of the films *A Hard Day's Night* and *Help!*, contacted him about writing a screenplay for the Beatles. Orton wrote in his diary:

> ...the Beatles are getting fed up with the Dick Lester type of direction. They want dialogue to speak... Difficult this as I don't think any of the Beatles can act in any accepted sense. As Marilyn Monroe couldn't. (15 January 1967)

From the beginning, Orton had doubts that the film would ever be made and was not going to exert himself unduly. He couldn't be bothered to write interesting new characters for the Beatles to play so noted in his diary that he would just write four variations on characters from *Entertaining Mr Sloane* and *Loot*:

After all if I repeat myself in this film it doesn't matter.
Nobody who sees the film will have seen *Sloane* or *Loot*.
(16 January)

On 24 January, Orton spent an evening at the house of Brian
Epstein, the Beatles' manager. There he discussed the film – as well
as theatre, pop music and drugs – with Paul McCartney. After the
meeting, Orton was more enthusiastic about the film but was
determined to be well-paid. The next day he arranged with Ramsay
that she would ask the Beatles for fifteen thousand pounds but would
accept twelve.

'If they won't pay us ten they can fuck themselves,' said Orton.

'Of course, darling,' replied Ramsay.

He drew heavily on his novel *The Vision of Gombold Proval* for the
Beatles script, which he called *Up Against It*. On 11 February, he met
Shenson for a final talk before the contracts were signed. Shenson
warned him: '... the boys shouldn't be made to do anything in the
film that would reflect badly on them.' Orton didn't have the heart to
tell him that, in his script, 'the boys' were adulterous murdering cross-
dressers who were put in prison for high treason.

Both Ramsay and Lewenstein were impressed by the completed
screenplay but the Beatles' office rejected it without explanation.
Orton's comment was brief and to the point: 'Fuck them.' The obvious
next move would have been to sell the script to the Rolling Stones.
Mick Jagger and his boys would have delighted in the shady goings-
on of *Up Against It* and were always keen to go where the Beatles
feared to tread. In fact, Lewenstein bought it for £10,000 and it remains
one of those Brigadoon screenplays which resurfaces periodically
amidst rumours that it is 'just about to be made.'

Orton had plenty of other work to occupy him. He was commissioned
by ITV to write the 'Charity' episode of a series called *The Seven
Deadly Virtues*. The result of this was *Funeral Games*. On 6 June
1967, *Crimes of Passion*, a double-bill comprising *The Ruffian on*

the Stair and *The Erpingham Camp*, opened at the Royal Court. His confidence was at a peak as he started work on what was to be his final play.

What the Butler Saw opened on 5 March 1969 at the Queen's Theatre, London. Its cast included Sir Ralph Richardson, Stanley Baxter, Julia Foster and Coral Browne. Richardson was baffled by the part of Dr Rance. Browne believes that he was so lost in speeches containing words like 'transvestite' and 'nymphomaniac' because he had no idea what those words meant. Orton had discussed the casting of Richardson with Lewenstein. He thought that Sir Ralph was 'a good ten years too old for the part.' On the opening night, Richardson was heckled with cries of 'Filth!' 'Give back your knighthood!' and 'Find another play!' Harold Hobson, writing in the *Sunday Times*, called the play 'a wholly unacceptable exploitation of sexual perversion.' Only Frank Marcus, in the *Sunday Telegraph*, saw that it would become 'a comedy classic of English literature.' This process did not begin until 1975 when Lindsay Anderson revived it at the Royal Court. It is Orton's best play and has become his most popular and widely performed work.

Orton did not live to see even a rehearsal of it.

The man he left behind

While Orton enjoyed life - meeting producers, reporters, actors and Paul McCartney - Halliwell stayed at home in their claustrophobic flat, fielding the phone calls that were always for Orton. His relationship with Orton had seen him progressively demoted. He had begun as Orton's teacher. He had become his partner. By the end, his official title for legal and financial purposes was 'Mr Orton's Personal Assistant'.

When Orton's mother died on 26 December 1966, it affected Halliwell more than it did Orton. Hearing the news did not stem Orton's creative flow. In his diary for 27 December, he reports: 'Today I did nothing but write *What the Butler Saw*.' Halliwell never got over the death of his own mother. He watched Orton effortlessly shrug off the event that had haunted him all his life. He now had yet another reason to be jealous.

Halliwell spent hours alone in the flat reading Orton's diaries. He was often referred to in them as just 'Kenneth Halliwell.' This was simply Orton's way of distinguishing him from Kenneth Williams, who had become a good friend of them both. But, to Halliwell, it seemed a cold and distant way of referring to one's lover. The diaries also contained explicit accounts of Orton's infidelities. Orton was rampantly promiscuous, both with the boys in Morocco and with men he picked up in London lavatories. His attitude was expressed in his words to Kenneth Williams: 'You must do whatever you like as long as you enjoy it and don't hurt anybody else.'

'I'm basically guilty about being a homosexual you see,' replied Williams.

Orton's response was unequivocal: 'Then you shouldn't be. Get yourself fucked if you want to. Get yourself anything you like. Reject all the values of society. And enjoy sex. When you're dead you'll regret not having fun with your genital organs.'

Orton did not follow all of his own injunctions. He did whatever he liked. He enjoyed it. But he did hurt somebody else. He hurt Halliwell, whose philosophy was the exact opposite of Orton's: 'You can only live properly if it's for one person or for God.' Halliwell felt threatened by the other men in Orton's life. He was embarrassed by his baldness and by his failure. He had no confidence in his looks, his worth or Orton's loyalty. He was terrified that Orton would leave him.

Initially, Halliwell sought the attention of the world, first as an actor, then as a writer. As late as 1966, he sent his stage adaptation, *The Facts of Life*, to Peggy Ramsay. She did not mince her words in her reply: 'I haven't really got through your adaptation. The first scene sent me into such a well of boredom that I had to struggle to continue which I did in a kind of abstract anguish!!!' She later said of the play: 'Unfortunately it wasn't any good. It was trying to be like one of Joe's, but it had no plot, no detail.' Towards the end, Halliwell would have been happy if just one person – Orton – had paid attention to him. He tried the usual tricks of the attention seeker – hypochondria, aggression, threatened suicide. Orton's diary tells the story:

> Kenneth has decided that what is wrong with him isn't his heart but his liver. He isn't eating. Just sipping milk every few hours. Most tiresome... As Kenneth has decided to go on hunger strike I shall now get all my own meals. This doesn't worry me particularly, except that it means we're starting to live quite separate lives. (2 April 1967)

> At 7.30 this morning Kenneth got up and made a cup of tea. I was hardly awake. I sat drinking my tea and began talking. Suddenly I realised that Kenneth was looking tight-lipped and white-faced. We were in the middle of talks of suicide and 'You'll have to face up to the world one day.' And 'I'm disgusted by all this immorality.' ... after a particularly sharp outburst, [he] alarmed me by saying, 'Homosexuals disgust me!' I didn't attempt to fathom this one out. He said he wasn't going to come away to Morocco. He was going to kill himself. 'I've led a dreadful, unhappy life. I'm pathetic. I can't go on suffering like this.' (2 May)

> When I got home, Kenneth H. was in such a rage. He'd written in large letters on the wall, 'JOE ORTON IS A SPINELESS TWAT.' (5 May)

The end

The diary entry for 27 June reports that while they were in Tangier, Halliwell attacked Orton for the first time:

> Kenneth became violently angry... and attacked me, hitting me about the head... 'And when we get back to London,' he said, 'we're finished. This is the end!' I had heard this so often. 'I wonder you didn't add "I'm going back to mother,"' I said wearily. 'That's the kind of line which makes your plays ultimately worthless,' he said. It went on

and on until I put the light out. He slammed the door and went to bed.

By July, Halliwell was throwing tantrums, screaming abuse at Orton and threatening suicide on a daily basis. Orton just kept on writing. He even managed to transform the atmosphere in the flat into the images of despair and entrapment in *What the Butler Saw* – the siren, the bars, the straitjackets. Success made Orton impervious to Halliwell's abuse. Halliwell could call Orton's plays 'ultimately worthless' but that could not alter the fact that Orton's plays were running in the West End while Halliwell's gathered dust on the shelf. Halliwell could not share Orton's success. What he could do was end it.

On 9 August 1967, while Orton was asleep, Halliwell killed him with nine hammer blows to the head. He then committed suicide by swallowing twenty-two Nembutals. He left a note which read:

> If you read his diary all will be explained.
> KH
> PS Especially the latter part.

He spent a lifetime trying to convince the world that he was important. Whether inadvertently or not, he achieved this end when he killed Orton. Orton's success had pushed him to the sidelines. Murder gave him centre stage. He ensured that any discussion of Joe Orton would have to devote considerable space to the life and opinions of Kenneth Halliwell. If Orton had left him or if he had killed just himself, he would have been merely a footnote in Orton's biography.

Orton was identified by his brother, Douglas. Ramsay identified Halliwell. Her comment was: 'I looked hard and felt nothing.' Halliwell was cremated on 17 August. Only Ramsay and three of his relatives were there. Orton's funeral was held the day after at the West Chapel of Golders Green Crematorium. His coffin disappeared through the hatch to the strains of his favourite song, The Beatles' 'A

Day in the Life':

> I read the news today oh boy
> About a lucky man who made the grade
> And though the news was rather sad
> Well I just had to laugh...

One of Halliwell's relatives suggested intermingling the two sets of ashes. Douglas Orton agreed with a proviso his brother would have enjoyed, one reminiscent of the last line of *Loot*: 'As long as nobody hears about it in Leicester.'

Chapter Two
The early plays

Orton's career as a playwright spanned just eight years. His development from *Fred and Madge* (1959) to *What the Butler Saw* (1967) was a rapid one. His early plays are those of a man unsure of his style, with a tendency to ape such literary forbears as Ronald Firbank and Harold Pinter. The later plays show him as a writer with a rapidly emerging voice of his own.

Fred and Madge

As his first play opens, Fred and Madge, a middle-aged couple, are discussing their boredom. Fred worries about growing old and reflects ruefully on what he could have made of his life. Madge's sister Queenie arrives. She and Madge discuss a group of people that sounds suspiciously like the royal family – but turns out to be characters from a soap opera. Webber enters. He is the play's director. He discusses the action with Sykes, one of the audience. He tells Sykes that he is engaged to Janice, Fred and Madge's daughter.

Fred goes to work. His job is an endless repetition of the task of Sisyphus: he pushes a boulder up a hill and then watches it roll down again. Madge is also working. Her job is to catch bath water in a sieve. Webber asks Sykes what he thinks of the show so far. Sykes responds that he'd like a drink so Webber makes several cuts to the play. Fred tells Madge that he's going to leave her. He also wants to smash the alarm clock that has been annoying him for so many years. Webber comes in to speed up their parting and then escorts Sykes to the bar.

Act Two opens as Webber and Sykes return from the bar discussing the plot. Nobody has heard from Fred since he and Madge divorced. Queenie is set to marry an Indian and plans to enter his harem in Sutpura. Fred and Madge meet unexpectedly when they find themselves in adjacent hospital beds. Fred is engaged to a sixteen year old, Madge to a sixty-one year old - who turns out to be Webber. As the arrangements are being made for Queenie's wedding, she hears that the Sunday papers are threatening to publish the story of her fiancé's murderous past. Webber tries to save her this embarrassment by hiring Harry Petrie and Grace Oldbourne, a professional insultor and insultrix. The papers will agree to keep quiet about the Indian's past if they can print the insults aimed at the wedding guests. Petrie and Oldbourne arrive and display their insulting prowess.

London is changing. Fred's father has, after a shaky start in the profession, proved so successful as a gardener that the parks and woods are engulfing the city. Coupled with this, Fred has discovered that buildings fall down if you laugh at them. He arranges for parties of laughers to destroy the great London monuments. Madge, meanwhile, has arranged to go off to India with Queenie.

By Act Three, Fred and Madge have remarried. They did it during a time-lapse so Madge failed to notice it. Fred has been trying to die but isn't up to it intellectually. He decides he might as well come with Madge and Queenie. The play ends with the characters imagining their new life in India.

Fred and Madge bears the hallmarks of a first attempt. There is little action. Almost everything is said rather than shown. It is self-indulgent. There is only a thin plot, which Orton happily abandons every time he goes on a new flight of fancy. Many of the lines are there simply because they are good lines, rather than because they advance the story or build up the characters. It is not really a play at all but a loosely connected series of sketches and jokes. This is a form of writing with a noble precedent. After all, what is *As You Like It* but a collection of all the scenes Shakespeare couldn't fit into his other plays?

Some of the ideas in *Fred and Madge* are unsophisticated. Orton always believed in the destructive power of comedy but gave this belief its crudest expression in the image of buildings toppling when people laugh at them. Other ideas work well. There is a lot of fun to be had with his blurring of the boundaries between stage time and real time. Sykes spends the interval in the theatre bar. Fifteen or twenty minutes is a reasonable length of time to spend in a bar. However, in the play, five years have passed between the end of Act One and the beginning of Act Two. So Sykes has spent five years in a bar. The cast becomes understandably worried about his drinking. Dramatic conventions are gleefully flouted. Webber and Sykes play a choric rôle in that they comment on the play's action. Traditionally, the chorus does not become directly involved in the action. Webber violates this tradition by becoming engaged to two of the play's characters.

The sort of deconstruction in which the people on stage make it clear that they know they're in a play was, according to C.W.E. Bigsby used by Orton again in *Entertaining Mr Sloane*. In his book, *Joe Orton*, Bigsby suggests that the characters in *Entertaining Mr Sloane* '... are purely theatrical figures – a status to which the text itself confesses.' His evidence for this claim is found in such lines as Kath's request to Sloane: 'Kiss my hand, dear, in the manner of the theatre.' (p143) A little later her brother, Ed, stops Sloane's attack on her with the words: 'This is gratuitous violence,' (p146) a term normally used only to talk about works of fiction. It would sound very odd to say there was a lot of gratuitous violence in the First World War. However, these lines do not constitute sufficient justification for saying that they are 'purely theatrical figures' or that they know they're in a play. It is more likely that Orton simply gave the characters dialogue which reflects the influence of popular theatre, film and television on their lives. The deconstruction in *Fred and Madge* is just the young Orton experimenting with a technique which he quickly rejected.

The influence of Ronald Firbank

The language used towards the end of *Fred and Madge*, particularly when Fred discusses India, is reminiscent of Firbank. Firbank's influence on Orton has sometimes been over-emphasised. Francesca Coppa, in her introduction to *Fred and Madge*, writes: '... in his adult diary, Orton refers to Firbank respectfully as "the source."' This is misleading as it suggests that Orton is acknowledging Firbank as the source of his own writing. The full quote from the diary is: 'I've read *Black Mischief* (patchy – Waugh isn't up to Firbank, the source)...' (25 March 1967) Orton is clearly saying that Firbank is the source of Waugh's work, rather than of his own. Firbank's extravagant, over-literary and ultimately tiresome style had a huge influence on Halliwell's writing. Peggy Ramsay wrote of Halliwell's *The Facts of Life*: 'What I've read reads like an adaptation from a novel, because the first speech is so damned *literary* and the speeches are nearly always written beyond their "holding" capacity.' Peter Willes, the producer of Orton's television plays, said of Halliwell's efforts: 'They were not like Joe's whatsoever. They were like very pseudo Ronald Firbank.' When he wrote *Fred and Madge*, Orton had not yet fully emerged from Halliwell's literary shadow. Consequently, his first play sees Fred going into Firbankian raptures about a fantasy India: 'We shall be the favourites of princes; ride in howdahs and palanquins; live in purple-hued throne rooms; dine off golden platters; listen to the music of flutes; watch the dancing of exotic slaves –' (p94) As Orton developed as a playwright, he began to shake off the Firbank influence. He did write out lists of Firbankian phrases - 'Windows like three orange eyes peering out of the fog,' 'A sea like luminous milk,' 'A cypress rose blackly out of a mist of olives,' – but it is significant that few of these phrases made it into the final drafts of his plays. Firbank was more of an influence on Orton's subject matter than on his style. Firbank often presented sexual perversion threatening to break through a veneer of respectability. This theme also appears frequently in Orton. Ed in *Entertaining Mr Sloane* is an upstanding man of affairs with an uncontrollable desire for young men. Pringle in *Funeral Games* is a man of God exposed as an adulterer. Dr Prentice in *What the Butler Saw* is a respected psychiatrist who is also a rapist. However, Orton soon learnt to present these themes in concise epigrams that would have been totally alien to Firbank. There is little trace of Firbank in the mature Orton's style.

The Visitors

Orton's second play is very different from *Fred and Madge*. In *The Visitors*, he abandons all theatrical games and playing with convention to present a straightforward slice of life drama.

Mrs Platt goes to the hospital to visit Kemp, her elderly father. Kemp is convinced that he's dying. Mrs Platt dismisses the suggestion with breezy cheerfulness. Meanwhile, the nurses in their common room discuss horse racing. They also bitch about Sister Marquand and each other. At the end of Act One, Nurse Cameron reveals that she's pregnant.

Kemp discusses family matters and radio plays with Basset, another patient. Sister scolds them both - Basset, for not having a bath; Kemp, for not having a bowel movement. Mrs Platt arrives. She, Kemp and Basset discuss the First World War, in which Kemp was wounded and decorated. Kemp wonders if his military service was worthwhile. Basset works at the Council Refuse Disposal Depot. Mrs Platt asks him if he gets a bath at work. Basset shows signs of personal hygiene paranoia: she's the second person today who's mentioned baths to him. As Mrs Platt is leaving, Kemp reminds her to be careful crossing the road. Nurse Sims comes in to tend to Kemp. They look out the window and see Mrs Platt being knocked down by a car.

In Act Three, it's Kemp's turn to visit Mrs Platt. They gossip about people they know and do their own bitching about Sister Marquand. Nurse Cameron tells her colleagues that she'll have to get married. She's just not sure if she loves the man who's made her pregnant. Kemp falls asleep in the chair by Mrs Platt's bed. There is commotion amongst the nurses when they're told he has passed out. The play ends with Mrs Platt realizing that her father is dead.

The Visitors has many of *Fred and Madge's* faults. There are pages of dialogue which establishes very little. Plot lines are opened and then not adequately explored or resolved. It struggles to reach a satisfactory ending.

Unfortunately, it does not have *Fred and Madge's* virtues - there is none of the outrageousness and playfulness that were to become Orton's trademarks. Nevertheless, it does offer some glimmers of what was to come. Mrs Platt and Kemp can be seen as a dry run for the characters of Kath and Kemp in *Entertaining Mr Sloane*. In each play, the character called Kemp is convinced that he's dying. In each play, nobody takes Kemp's fears seriously:

KEMP: I shall be here until they carry me out.
MRS PLATT: We'll have you skipping about in no time!
KEMP: I won't bother you much longer.
MRS PLATT: I won't have that kind of talk, do you hear? You've got years ahead of you. What do you want to die for?
(p103, *The Visitors*, Act One)

KEMP: I'm going to die, Kath... I'm dying.
KATH: (*angrily*) You've been at the ham haven't you? Half a jar of pickles you've put away. Don't moan to me if you're up half the night with the tummy ache. I've got no sympathy for you.
(p92, *Entertaining Mr Sloane*, Act One)

Both Mrs Platt and Kath are convinced that nothing is more efficacious than toffee in the treatment of the sick and elderly:

MRS PLATT: (*rummaging in a hold-all*) I brought you these. (*Produces a tin of toffee.*) I know you're not supposed to have them, but I thought you'd like to.
KEMP: I don't know.
MRS PLATT: I'll just slip them under your pillow. (*Doing so.*) Something sweet, that's what you need to keep your pecker up.
(p99, *The Visitors,* Act One)

In *Entertaining Mr Sloane*, Kath's comment on being told that Kemp is recovering from a brutal kicking is: 'I'd take up a toffee, but he only gets them stuck round his teeth.' (p129)

Mrs Platt and Kath both employ babytalk when addressing their fathers. Mrs Platt asks her father: 'Have a grape? Grapie? A little one?' (p102) Kath tells hers: 'Go to bed. I'll bring you a drinkie.' (p92)

One of the images in *Entertaining Mr Sloane* is lifted directly from *The Visitors*. Mrs Platt says of Sister Marquand: 'I suppose she'll be in in a minute with that bell of hers. What with that and the crows' feet round her eyes, it makes her an object of terror.' (p154) Kath's brother tells her: 'You're fat and the crows-feet under your eyes would make you an object of terror.' (p143)

The character of the Catholic nurse, O'Hara, hints at Orton's interest in sex seen in the light of Catholic tradition. O'Hara's response to the nurses' dream of Sister Marquand getting pregnant is: 'It would have to be an Immaculate Conception. No man would touch her.' (p161) This interest had become a fascination by the time Orton wrote *Loot*, in which two young men discuss the proclivities of another Catholic nurse, Fay:

HAL: She's three parts Papal nuncio. She'd only do it at set times.
DENNIS: Oh, no. She does it at any time. A typical member of the medical profession she is.
HAL: You've had her? (DENNIS *grins*.) Knocked it off? Really?
DENNIS: Under that picture of the Sacred Heart.
(p210, *Loot*, Act One)

A little earlier, Hal tells Fay that his father gave more time to his flowers than he gave to his wife:

HAL: If she'd played her cards right, my mother could've cited the Rose Growers' Annual as co-respondent.
FAY: The Vatican would never grant an annulment. Not unless he'd produced a hybrid. (p199)

The Ruffian on the Stair

Neither *Fred and Madge* nor *The Visitors* was performed in Orton's lifetime. His next play marked the beginning of his success. *The Ruffian on the Stair* was performed both on radio and on stage.

Joyce, a woman with a mysterious past, reads that a man called Frank has been run over by a van and killed. After her lover, Mike, has gone out to meet some of his shady business associates, a young man arrives to inquire about a room to let. This man, Wilson, is Frank's brother. He believes that Frank was murdered. He knows a surprising amount about Joyce and her relationship with Mike. Wilson becomes aggressive and asks if Mike would avenge an assault on Joyce. He knows that Mike has a gun. He finds it and assures himself that it's loaded.

He leaves but returns the next day when Mike is at home. Joyce complains that Wilson has been harassing her but Mike wants to hear Wilson's side of the story. He invites Wilson in. Wilson says that he has been suicidal since his brother's death. He accuses Mike of having taken money to kill Frank. He then taunts Mike by claiming to have slept with Joyce. Mike threatens Wilson with the gun. Wilson responds: 'The heart is situated... just below the badge on my pullover. Don't miss, will you? I don't want to be injured. I want to be dead.' (p54). By making Mike kill him, thereby forcing Mike to face a murder charge, Wilson will avenge his brother's death. He leaves. Mike threatens to murder Joyce for her infidelity with Wilson but relents because he doesn't want to be alone.

The next morning, Wilson comes into the room while Mike is downstairs. Wilson unmasks Joyce as a former prostitute. He claims Frank was one of her clients. Wilson starts to undress so that Mike will catch them apparently in flagrante. Joyce is melted by Wilson's tale of his heartbreak over his brother's death. She embraces him. Mike enters, sees them wrapped around each other and fires two shots, one of which hits Wilson in the chest and kills him. Joyce promises to stand by Mike and to tell the police that Wilson assaulted her. She discovers that the other shot has shattered the goldfish bowl and killed her goldfish. The play ends as Mike goes out with the words: 'I'll fetch the police. This has been a crime of passion. They'll understand. They have wives and goldfish of their own.' (p61)

The Ruffian on the Stair is more poignant than Orton's later plays. The characters in *Loot* and *What the Butler Saw* selfishly pursue their own ends and see other people merely as a means or a hindrance to those ends. Mike and Wilson have real feelings. Mike is afraid of loneliness so wants to be with Joyce whatever she's done. Wilson is desperately unhappy about his brother's death:

WILSON: I wasn't with him when he died. I'm going round the twist with heartbreak.
MIKE: He's dead?
WILSON: Yes. I thought of topping myself...
MIKE: Kill yourself?
WILSON: I don't want to live, see.
(p50)

Later, he tells Joyce: 'I'm sorry if I've caused trouble. I'm not usually like this. My heart is breaking. I wish I'd been with him when he died.' (p60) Such human emotion is unusual for an Orton character. In *Loot*, for example, Hal is altogether more sanguine about his mother's death:

MCLEAVY: (*to* HAL) Where are your tears? She was your mother.
HAL: It's dust, Dad.
    MCLEAVY *shakes his head in despair.*
A little dust.
(p263)

There is another reason for the strength of Wilson's feelings for his brother. There is a strong suggestion that the affection between them went beyond the purely fraternal:

34

WILSON: ... We were bosom friends. I've never told anyone that before. I hope I haven't shocked you.

MIKE: As close as that?

WILSON: We had separate beds - he was a stickler for convention, but that's as far as it went. We spent every night in each other's company. It was the reason we never got any work done.

MIKE: There's no word in the Irish language for what you were doing.

(p49-50)

Incest is a recurrent theme in Orton's plays. Freud saw it as an image of anarchy so it's not surprising that it interested such an anarchic playwright. In *Entertaining Mr Sloane*, Sloane has a sexual relationship with Kath. She had her baby son taken away from her and there are hints that that baby may have grown up to be Sloane. He is the same age as her son and resembles the baby's father:

SLOANE: You're not alone.

KATH: I am. (*Pause.*) Almost alone. (*Pause.*) If I'd been allowed to keep my boy I'd not be. (*Pause.*) You're almost the same age as he would be. You've got the same refinement.

(p68)

KATH:... I was trying to find the letter from my little boy's father. I treasure it. But I seem to have mislaid it. I found a lot of photos though... Are you interested in looking through them? (*Brings the snapshots over.*)

SLOANE: Are they him?

KATH: My lover.

SLOANE: Bit blurred.

KATH: It brings back memories. He reminds me of you...

(p93-4)

In his later plays, there is more explicit anarchy as Orton reveals the corruption of authority figures. The police are easily bribed in *Loot*. The Church is a hotbed of adulterers and murderers in *Funeral Games*.

And in *What the Butler Saw*, the two presentations of anarchy come together - the head of the psychiatric clinic is a lying adulterer, the policeman happily assists in covering up wrongdoings *and* four of the six characters commit incest.

The influence of Harold Pinter

Orton substantially rewrote the radio version of *The Ruffian on the Stair* as part of the 1967 Royal Court show, *Crimes of Passion*. When Harold Pinter read the rewrite, he told Orton: 'You're a bloody marvellous writer.' It's not hard to see why the play appealed to him. Orton's early plays were much influenced by Pinter, who was described by John Lahr as 'The only contemporary English playwright besides himself that Orton admired.' On almost every page of *The Ruffian on the Stair* and *Entertaining Mr Sloane*, Pinter's favourite stage direction - (*Pause.*) – appears like a rash. It is used more sparingly in *Loot* and hardly ever appears in *Funeral Games* or *What the Butler Saw*.

For *The Ruffian on the Stair*, Orton drew on two of Pinter's plays – *The Room* and *The Birthday Party*. The basic situation is derived from *The Room*. Each play features a woman, left alone by her partner in a flat, being visited by a strange man who seems to know her. However, in *The Room*, it is never explained who Riley is, how he knows Rose or what he wants with her. The rest of the play is taken up with rather aimless dialogue between Rose and a couple who may, or may not, be moving into the same building. By contrast, in *The Ruffian on the Stair*, Wilson is the brother of the man murdered by Mike; he knows Joyce because his brother used to visit her; he wants Joyce to be the instrument of his own death and of vengeance for his brother. It seems that Orton read *The Room* and wondered what it would be like if it had a plot and made sense.

The dialogue of *The Ruffian on the Stair* owes much to *The Birthday Party*. In the original radio version, Orton opens with a scene at the breakfast table:

JOYCE: Did you enjoy your breakfast?

MIKE: What?

JOYCE: Did you enjoy your breakfast? The egg was nice, wasn't it? The eggs are perfect now that I have the timer. Have you noticed? (*Pause.*) The marmalade was nice. Did it go down well?

MIKE: The egg was nice...

Lahr accuses Orton of stealing this scene from Pinter. This is pitching it too strong but Orton was certainly influenced by:

MEG: I've got your cornflakes ready. (*She disappears and reappears.*) Here's your cornflakes.
> *He rises and takes the plate from her, sits at the table, props up the paper and begins to eat. Meg enters by the kitchen door.*

Are they nice?

PETEY: Very nice.

MEG: I thought they'd be nice...

(*The Birthday Party,* Act One)

When *The Ruffian on the Stair* was rewritten for the stage, the opening had been changed to something distinctively Ortonesque:

JOYCE: Have you got an appointment today?

MIKE: Yes. I'm to be at King's Cross station at eleven. I'm meeting a man in the toilet.

...

JOYCE: You always go to such interesting places.

(p31)

Anything about meeting men in toilets shows Orton writing straight from the heart. One thing that does survive in the stage version is a Pinteresque interrogation:

WILSON: It was on October the twenty-first he was killed. What were you doing that day?

MIKE: I was fishing.

...

WILSON: Did you have the good fortune to find a salmon on the end of your line?

MIKE: No. Whoever heard of catching salmon in a canal?

WILSON: You killed my brother.

(p52)

This technique of disorientating the accused with questions about trivia is frequently used in Pinter. Notably:

GOLDBERG: ... When did you last have a bath?

STANLEY: I have one every-

GOLDBERG: Don't lie.

MCCANN: You betrayed the organization. I know him!

(*The Birthday Party,* Act Two)

Both *The Ruffian on the Stair* and *Entertaining Mr Sloane* have the basic situation that the arrival of a stranger has a great impact on a tranquil home. This situation is repeated many times in Pinter - Goldberg and McCann arriving in *The Birthday Party*, Riley in *The Room*, Davies in *The Caretaker*, Ruth in *The Homecoming*.

Entertaining Mr Sloane also draws on *The Birthday Party*. Each play features a woman who combines maternal feelings with sexual desire in her attitude to a younger man. Orton is a good deal more explicit in his treatment of this situation. Whereas Kath is seen seducing Sloane on stage and is later revealed to be pregnant with his child, Pinter merely hints at a sexual relationship between Meg and Stanley:

STANLEY: ... I need a new room!

MEG: (*sensual, stroking his arm*) Oh, Stan, that's a lovely room. I've had

some lovely afternoons in that room.

(*The Birthday Party*, Act One)

In each play, the young man responds with aggressive disdain. Kath warns Sloane about the dangers of picking up a loose woman:

KATH: She'll make you ill.

...

SLOANE: How dare you. Making filthy insinuations. I won't have it. You disgust me you do. Standing there without your teeth. Why don't you get smartened up? Get a new rig out.

(p99)

This outburst is reminiscent of Stanley's violent speech to Meg: 'Look, why don't you get this place cleared up! It's a pigsty. And another thing, what about my room? It needs sweeping. It needs papering...'
(*The Birthday Party*, Act One) Despite their age, both Kath and Meg believe themselves to be still attractive. Each woman seeks the approval of the dominant male – Kath of her brother Ed, Meg of Goldberg.

There are also similarities between these two men. Each man sets great store by his 'position':

MCCANN: That's a great compliment, Nat, coming from a man in your position.

GOLDBERG: Well, I've got a position, I won't deny it.

(*The Birthday Party*, Act One)

In a similar vein, Ed tells Kath: 'You've got to realize my position... Some of my associates are men of distinction. They think nothing of tipping a fiver.' (p82) They both reminisce about bygone days of innocence. Goldberg recalls: 'When I was a youngster, of a Friday, I used to go for a walk down the canal with a girl who lived down my road... Good? Pure? She wasn't a Sunday school teacher for nothing.'
(*The Birthday Party*, Act Two) Ed has similar, though less

heterosexual, nostalgia for the past: 'I had a matie. What times we had. Fished. Swam. Rolled home pissed at two in the morning. We were innocent I tell you.' (p114)

Orton took some of Pinter's ideas and dramatic techniques and fed them into more classically structured works. Pinter's plays offer the audience a slice of the life of rather bizarre characters whose motives are often obscure. His plays rarely arrive at a natural ending in which it is made clear how the characters have been changed by the events. This reflects real life but it can make for an unsatisfying night at the theatre. Orton was, in some ways, more conservative. After trying out different dramatic forms in *Fred and Madge* and *The Visitors*, he became convinced that a play must have a plot. In *The Ruffian on the Stair* and *Entertaining Mr Sloane*, there is clear declaration of the characters' motives and a logical, if unexpected, conclusion – literary conceits for which Pinter has no time.

Chapter Three
Entertaining Mr Sloane

After Orton's first meeting with Peggy Ramsay, she rang Michael Codron and told him: 'I've just met a very promising writer, and he's living on £3 10s a week. Will you read his play immediately?' That play was *Entertaining Mr Sloane*. It was the first of Orton's plays to reach the stage. It was also his first major work. It remains one of the plays – along with *Loot* and *What the Butler Saw* – on which his reputation rests.

The middle-aged Kath meets a young man, Sloane, in the library. She invites him to move into her spare room. Some years ago, Kath had her only baby taken away from her. She wants Sloane to replace him. Sloane's presence is resented by Kath's father, Kemp. Kemp's employer was murdered by a man answering to Sloane's description. He accuses Sloane of the crime and lunges at him with a toasting fork. Kath tends to the wound in Sloane's leg and takes the opportunity to entice him out of his trousers. Kath's brother, Ed, arrives and tells her that people will talk if they know she has a young man in the house. He intends asking Sloane to leave but, when he meets him, is instantly consumed with lust. He offers Sloane a job as his chauffeur. After Ed leaves, Kath puts on a transparent négligée and seduces Sloane.

Some months later, Sloane is settled in the house and happily plays Kath and Ed off against each other to get his own way. Kath reveals that she's pregnant and tries to persuade Sloane to marry her. Sloane refuses marriage but gives her his locket as a token of his esteem. Ed confronts Sloane about his misdemeanours. Sloane has been joy-riding with women in Ed's car, has got his sister pregnant and has been harassing his father. But Ed is so enamoured with Sloane that he responds: 'Your youth pleads for leniency and, by God, I'm going to give it. You're as pure as the lamb. Purer.' (p120) Ed leaves Sloane and Kemp to sort matters out between themselves. They quarrel. Sloane kicks Kemp to death.

Ed and Kath agree to tell the authorities that Kemp fell down the stairs. Ed arranges that Sloane should move in with him. Kath says that if Sloane moves out, she will tell the police the truth about Kemp's death. Ed counters by saying that if Sloane does not move in with him, then he will go to the police. He tells Sloane: 'It's what is called a dilemma, boy. You are on the horns of it.' (p145) Ed and Kath agree to treat Sloane like a timeshare villa in Marbella. They will each have him for half a year. Ed takes the locket Sloane gave Kath as a symbol of his ownership of Sloane for the next six months.

A new breed of homosexual

When *Entertaining Mr Sloane* first appeared, audiences were surprised and disconcerted by Orton's portrayal of Ed. He was not the sort of gay man they were used to seeing on stage. He was neither an extravagant music hall drag queen nor an unhappy young man for whom homosexuality is a problem like, for example, Geof in Shelagh Delaney's *A Taste of Honey* (1958.) Orton stipulated that Ed must be played as an 'attractive masculine man.' He is the assertive head of his family: his father and sister are both a little afraid of him. He has a good job, two cars and enough money to employ a chauffeur. He conceals his passions behind his image as an upstanding man of affairs. He isn't honest about his sexuality. He has not come out, even to himself. He is very open about his dislike of women:

ED: ... I live in a world of top decisions. We've no time for ladies.
KATH: Ladies are nice at a gathering.
ED: We don't want a lot of half-witted tarts.
(p90)

He is less candid about his feelings towards young men. He hides his interest behind a veneer of respectable philanthropy. He asks Sloane: 'Why am I interested in your welfare? Why did I give you a job?

Why do thinking men everywhere show young boys the strait and narrow?' (p134) If he were being honest, he would answer himself: 'Because I, and thinking men everywhere, want to get young boys into bed.' What he actually replies is: 'Principles, boy, bleeding principles. And don't you dare say otherwise or you'll land in serious trouble.'

Sloane has too much sense to say otherwise. After the murder of Kemp, Sloane needs Ed so he continues to play the game he has been playing since they met - Ed's game. He tells him: 'A couple of years ago I met a man similar to yourself... During the course of one magical night he talked to me of his principles - offered me a job if I would accept them. Like a fool I turned him down. What an opportunity I lost, Ed. If you were to make the same demands, I'd answer loudly in the affirmative.' (p135)

Ed covers his sexual desire for Sloane by seeking to be a father figure. Sloane realizes this. When Ed questions him about his shenanigans with Kath and Kemp, he defends himself by saying: 'It's my upbringing. Lack of training. No proper parental control.' (p119) Ed responds to this immediately:

ED: Why didn't you come to me?
SLOANE: It's not the kind of thing I could –
ED: I'd've been your confessor.
(p119-20)

The fantasy figure
Throughout the play, Sloane understands that he can get the most out of Ed by being whatever Ed wants him to be. When they first meet, Sloane presents himself as the realization of all Ed's fantasies:

ED: She [Kath] married a mate of mine – a valiant man – we were together in Africa.
SLOANE: In the army?

When Sloane asks this, apparently casual, question, Ed immediately breaks off his story about Kath's past to see if Sloane shares his militaristic fetish. Sloane is not going to disappoint him:

ED: You're interested in the army, eh? Soldiers, garrison towns, etc. Does that interest you?
SLOANE: Yes.
(p85)

A little later, Ed probes him again:

ED: You're fond of swimming?
SLOANE: I like a plunge now and then.
ED: Bodybuilding?
SLOANE: We had a nice little gym at the orphanage. Put me in all the teams they did.
...
ED: I used to do a lot of that at one time. With my mate... we used to do all what you've just said. (*Pause*). We were young. Innocent too. (*Shrugs. Pats his pocket. Takes out a packet of cigarettes. Smokes.*) All over now. (*Pause.*) Developing your muscles, eh? And character. (*Pause.*) ... Well, well, well. (*Breathless.*) A little bodybuilder are you? I bet you are... (Slowly.) do you... (*Shy.*) exercise regular?
SLOANE: As clockwork.
ED: Good, good. Stripped?
SLOANE: Fully.
ED: Complete. (*Striding to the window.*) How invigorating.
...
ED: Do you wear leather... next to the skin? Leather jeans, say? Without... aah...
SLOANE: Pants?
ED: (laughs) Get away!
(p86-7)

Ed is breathless, restless, smoking with excitement. He has found a young man built from his own blueprints. And by employing Sloane as a chauffeur, he can dress him in a fantasy outfit:

ED: ... I could get you a uniform. Boots, pants, a guaranteed 100 per cent no imitation jacket... an... er... a white brushed nylon T-shirt... with a little leather cap. (*Laughs.*) Like that?
      SLOANE *nods.*
(p88)

Sloane profits at once from accommodating Ed's tastes. Ed allows him to stay in Kath's house and gives him a job. Ed is prepared to spend money on keeping Sloane near him. He tells Kath: 'Don't take any money from him. I'll pay.' (p89)

Sloane is a social chameleon. Who he is depends on who is with him. He is just as ready to fulfil Kath's emotional needs. Even though he assures Ed that he has no interest in women...

ED: ... Women are like banks, boy, breaking and entering is a serious business. Give me your word you're not vaginalatrous?
SLOANE: I'm not.
(p88)

... he nevertheless allows Kath to seduce him as soon as Ed is out of the house. Kath also has twin designs on Sloane. As Orton put it in a letter to Alan Schneider, she 'stalks his cock.' She also wants to mother him. The two desires are closely linked in her. She begins by trying to adopt Sloane as a surrogate son. As soon as he realizes this, he leaps in with an appeal to her maternal instincts:

SLOANE: I never had no family of my own.
KATH: Didn't you?
SLOANE: No. I was brought up in an orphanage.

She then kisses him on the cheek with the words: 'Just a motherly kiss. A real mother's kiss.' It isn't long, however, until she reveals intentions that would get her drummed out of any branch of the Mothers' Union:

KATH: I've been doing my washing today and I haven't a stitch on... except my shoes... I'm in the rude under this dress. I tell you because you're bound to have noticed...

...

    SLOANE *takes the nylon stocking from between cushions of the settee.*

I wondered where I'd left it.

SLOANE: Is it yours?

KATH: Yes. You'll notice the length? I've got long legs. Long, elegant legs. (*Kicks out her leg.*) I could give one or two of them a surprise. (*Pause.*) My look is quite different when I'm in private. (*Leans over him.*) You can't see through this dress can you? I been worried for fear of embarrassing you.

(p78)

At the end of Act One, the two desires come together:

KATH: ... I don't think the fastening on this thing I'm wearing will last much longer... (*Pause: he attempts to move; she is almost on top of him.*) Mr Sloane... (*Rolls on to him.*) You should wear more clothes, Mr Sloane. I believe you're as naked as me. And there's no excuse for it. (*Silence.*) I'll be your mamma. I need to be loved. Gently. Oh! I shall be so ashamed in the morning. (*Switches off the light.*) What a big heavy baby you are. Such a big heavy baby.

(p95)

Murder turns the tables

By satisfying Kath's needs, Sloane gets to stay in her house and enjoy her cooking. By satisfying Ed's, he gets a very understanding boss who forgives him everything and gives him two pay rises within the first few months of employment. This happy state of affairs could have continued indefinitely. Sloane, however, overplays his hand. He is convinced that Kath and Ed are so devoted to him that he can continue to control them even after he has murdered their father. He appeals to Ed:

SLOANE: Say he fell downstairs.
ED: What kind of person does that make me?
SLOANE: A loyal friend.
...
Are you going to help me?
ED: No.
(p134)

Sloane is forced to drop part of his facade. Up to this point, he has been concealing the calculating way in which he has been fulfilling Ed's dreams. His message to Ed so far has not been 'I can *become* the man you want,' but 'I *already am* the man you want.' He has presented himself as Ed's ready-made ideal. He now tells Ed baldly that he will become anything that Ed desires. If Ed helps him to escape the law, he will play any rôle Ed wants him to play:

SLOANE: Let me live with you. I'd wear my jeans out in your service. Cook for you.
ED: I eat out.
SLOANE: Bring you your tea in bed.
ED: Only women drink tea in bed.
SLOANE: You bring me my tea in bed, then. Any arrangement you fancy.
(p135)

Now that Sloane is in trouble and under threat of Ed's help being withdrawn, he openly admits that he will be a devoted slave or a pampered pet, whichever way Ed's fantasy moves him.

By this point, he has so little respect for Kath that it does not occur to him that she could be a threat. He does not know that she is finally prepared to assert herself. She first tells him that he must stay to take care of their baby. This doesn't work: Sloane has no interest in his responsibilities. The murder of Kemp allows Kath to threaten Sloane with something that does interest him - a prison sentence: 'I was never subtle, Mr Sloane... If you go with Eddie, I'll tell the police.' (p145)

When he realizes that Kath does have the power to hurt him, Sloane aims his first counter attack at her motherly side. Throughout the play, Kath refers to herself as Sloane's 'mamma.' Only now does Sloane call her this: 'Look - mamma... see -' (p144) When this tactic fails, the obvious next move for him would be a sexual approach. Ed's presence frustrates this move so he resorts to violence, slapping Kath and shaking her. When Ed steps in to stop the attack, Sloane shouts desperately: 'She's won! The bitch has won!' (p146) If Kath has won, the victory is not so much over Sloane as over Ed. Until now, Ed's complete dominance of Kath is never questioned. She accepts that he has the power even to turn her guests out of her house:

KATH: ... Ed, you won't tell him to go?
ED: (*brushing her aside*). Go and fetch him.
KATH: I'm not misbehaving. Ed, if you send him away I shall cry.
ED: (*raising his voice*). Let's have less of it. I'll decide.
(p82)

Kath stands up to Ed for the first time. He wants to take Sloane away with him. Kath will make trouble if he does. But has she 'won'? Orton didn't think so. On 2 October 1965, he wrote to Halliwell about the New York production:

> Last night when she [Kath] said 'It's murder' to SLOANE
> in the third act someone nearly said 'Atta girl!' - of course
> they imagine that this is the point where the action turns

and the tide runs in her favour ending up with her winning. Imagine their disbelief when EDDIE wins!

Orton should know but it's by no means certain that Ed wins either. Kath and Ed reach a compromise. Neither will turn Sloane over to the police if they both agree to share him:

ED: You've had him for six months; I'll have him the next six. I'm not robbing you of him permanently.
...
KATH: That's too long, dear. I get so lonely.
ED: I've got no objections if he visits you from time to time. Briefly. We could put it in the contract. Fair enough?
KATH: Yes.
ED: I'd bring him over myself in the car. Now, you'll be more or less out of action for the next three months. So shall we say next August? Agreed?
KATH: Perfect, Eddie. It's very clever of you to have thought of such a lovely idea!
ED: Put it down to my experience at the conference table.
(p148-9)

This does not sound like a victory for Ed or, indeed, for Kath. This sounds like a score draw. Even if there is no clear winner, there is a clear loser - Sloane. The murder of Kemp has transformed him from the controller into the controlled. The double meaning of the play's title emerges. Before the murder, Kath and Ed strain every nerve in their efforts to entertain Mr Sloane. After the murder, Mr Sloane becomes highly entertaining.

Totally heartless?

In his paper, 'Joe Orton: The Comedy of (Ill) Manners,' Martin Esslin draws a comparison between *Entertaining Mr Sloane* and Pinter's *The Caretaker*. He comments: '...whereas in *The Caretaker* the situation is invested with genuine pathos, both in Aston's need for a companion and in Davies's for a home, so that there is a real feeling of human suffering and tragedy behind even the most grotesquely deprived and ludicrously incompetent characters, the atmosphere of *Entertaining Mr Sloane* is totally heartless.' This is not entirely true. Certainly, Sloane and Ed are heartless characters. Sloane is psychotic. He has no qualms about using people for his own ends and, when he kills Kemp, feels no remorse, only fear about what will happen *to him* if his crime is discovered. Ed shows no evidence of genuine emotion. All his actions are guided by his two, somewhat incompatible, impulses – his need to keep up a respectable appearance and his desire for young men. Kath, on the other hand, generates genuine pathos. She was in love many years ago with Tommy, one of Ed's friends. She claims that they would have been married but Tommy's family objected. Ed's version of the story is that Tommy never loved her and never wanted to marry her. Either way, she clings to the memory of her lost love. She still keeps Tommy's photograph and the last letter he sent her – or, at least, she thinks she does until Ed disabuses her:

KATH: Did you burn my letter?
ED: Yes. (*Pause.*) And that old photo as well. I thought you was taking an unhealthy interest in the past.
(p108)

Whatever Tommy thought of her, she genuinely loved him. She also feels genuinely distraught about losing her baby. She first tells Sloane that her baby died, '... killed in very sad circumstances. It broke my heart at the time.' (p65) She later changes her story to say that the baby was adopted. The mystery that surrounds Kath's past can be seen as an indication of her grief. She makes up stories about the past to make it more bearable. She would not do that unless she had real feelings. She may have impure designs on Sloane's body, but there is real pathos in her desire for him to replace her child.

Orton's portrayal of Kath shows signs of ambivalence. He sets her up as a sympathetic character - a woman who has suffered losses that most audience members have suffered or can imagine suffering. He then undercuts that sympathy by making her disgusting. People may feel sorry for her but they will inevitably feel queasy at the spectacle of a forty-one year old woman seducing a man young enough to be her son - especially after the veiled hints that he might actually be her son. Sloane 'shudders a little' when Kath first touches his neck and his cheek. At one point she 'sniffs without dignity.' At another she blows her nose on her apron. Sloane and Ed are not shy about telling her how unattractive she is:

KATH: Do I disgust you?
SLOANE: Yes.
KATH: Honest?
SLOANE: And truly. You horrify me.
(p99)

ED: Look in the glass, lady. Let's enjoy a laugh. (*He takes her to the mirror.*) What do you see?
...
KATH: My hair is nice. Natural. I'm mature, but still able to command a certain appeal.
ED: You look like death!
(p142)

It's not too surprising that Orton portrays the homosexual relationship as more aesthetically pleasing than the heterosexual. Sloane and Ed are both – at least physically – attractive men. Kath is, by turns, pathetic, disgusting and predatory.

If Kath is unattractive it is because Orton based her on an unattractive figure from his past. When his sister Leonie saw Beryl Reid as Kath in the 1975 Royal Court revival, her first comment was: 'That's my mum! That's her! It's like seeing a ghost.'

The strength of *Entertaining Mr Sloane* lies in its dialogue. It is a very good play to read. It can be dull on the stage as there are long periods with no action in which the characters just sit about talking to each other. At this point in his career, Orton had not fully learnt how to move his characters round the stage. He began the process of letting his characters express themselves through action as well as dialogue in *Loot* and *Funeral Games*. He had the technique perfected by the time of *What the Butler Saw*.

Chapter Four
Loot

Loot is set in a house of mourning. Mrs Mary McLeavy is laid out in a coffin in the front room. She leaves behind her husband and her bisexual son, Hal. Also in the house is her nurse, Fay. Fay has had seven husbands so far and is keen to make Mr McLeavy her eighth. McLeavy reads in the newspaper that the local bank has been broken into by thieves who burrowed in from the undertaker's next door. Dennis, Hal's friend who works for the undertaker, arrives to collect the corpse. He and Hal have robbed the bank and have hidden the money in the wardrobe in McLeavy's front room. Dennis has had a visit from Inspector Truscott of the Yard and wants to get the money away. They decide to hide the money in the coffin. As there is no room in it for both money and corpse, they put Mrs McLeavy in the wardrobe with plans to dispose of her later.

Truscott comes to the house, posing as the man from the water board. He recognizes Fay and questions her about her husbands' violent deaths. He asks for a sample of her handwriting so she signs a page of his notebook.

Fay reveals to McLeavy that his wife changed her will just before she died, leaving Fay all her money. Fay says that she wants to give the money to McLeavy. The only way this can be managed without causing scandal is for him to marry her. This arrangement will, coincidentally, also give Fay access to McLeavy's money. Dennis has been sleeping with Fay and wants to marry her. As he's leaving with the coffin for the funeral, he tells her that he is richer than McLeavy. Fay is intrigued and decides not to attend the funeral. Hal also refuses to attend and, when they are alone, she persuades him to open the wardrobe where she finds the corpse. He offers to split the money with her if she strips the corpse for him. (Mrs McLeavy was to have been buried in her WVS uniform, which would make her too easy to identify.) As they are removing the corpse from the wardrobe, a glass eye drops from it and rolls away. They remove Mrs McLeavy's clothes and wrap her in a mattress cover. Truscott reappears. They tell him that the wrapped corpse is a tailor's dummy. He suspects Hal of being involved in the bank robbery and asks him where the money is. Hal, who has a pathological need to tell the truth, says that it's being buried by Father Jellicoe. Truscott doesn't believe him so knocks him to the floor and starts kicking him.

McLeavy comes in, heavily bandaged. He explains that the funeral cortège was hit by a lorry and the hearse destroyed. Hal and Dennis bring in the charred coffin. As they set it down, one of its sides falls off to reveal the money inside. Dennis stands in front of the coffin to hide the banknotes from Truscott and McLeavy. As the wreaths have all been destroyed, McLeavy and Truscott go off to fetch a picture of the Pope. Hal, Dennis and Fay decide to remove the money from the coffin and replace it with the corpse. Fay tells Dennis that, as he now has more money than McLeavy, she will marry him. Truscott returns, tells Dennis to take the corpse outside and then finds the glass eye.

In Act Two, Hal and Dennis come in, carrying the corpse. Truscott is so bemused by all the antics with a tailor's dummy that he threatens to arrest everyone. At this point, he admits that he is not from the water board but is in fact the legendary Truscott of the Yard. (He was forced into the deception by a legal anomaly which states that the police need a warrant to enter a private house but men from the water board don't.) He asks if Mrs McLeavy had any final words. Hal says she spoke of a book with a broken binding on McLeavy's shelf. The book turns out to be *The Trial of Phyllis McMahon*, the record of one of Truscott's cases – the case of a nurse accused of murdering a patient. The book contains a sample of the nurse's handwriting. It is identical to Fay's signature on the page of Truscott's notebook. Fay confesses that she poisoned Mrs McLeavy. Truscott asks for a sample of Mrs McLeavy's stomach to confirm Fay's story. All of Mrs McLeavy's internal organs were removed when she was embalmed. They were placed in a casket. In the crash that destroyed the hearse, the casket was forced open and the viscera destroyed. Without Mrs McLeavy's stomach, Truscott has no evidence so he releases Fay.

He then asks McLeavy about the glass eye. McLeavy suspects his son of having stolen parts of Mrs McLeavy and demands that the coffin be opened. When he lifts the lid, he sees the money and collapses. Truscott assumes it's the shock of seeing the corpse. He has no desire to see human remains so asks for the lid to be replaced without looking inside. Truscott and McLeavy go off. Hal, Dennis and Fay put the money into the casket. When Truscott returns, however, he says he'll take the casket with him when he leaves. As he lifts it up, the money falls to the floor. Hal bribes Truscott, agreeing to give him a quarter of the money. McLeavy is outraged by this display of police corruption and threatens to expose them all. Hal proposes that Truscott arrest McLeavy. This seems to be the best solution for everyone. Fay suggests that McLeavy's accidental death might be arranged in prison. The play ends with their arranging to bury McLeavy with his wife.

In 'Joe Orton: The Comedy of (Ill) Manners,' Esslin argues: 'Orton's rage is purely negative, it is unrelated to any positive creed, philosophy or programme of social reform.' At first sight, this appears to be a fair comment on *Loot*. The main target of his rage here is the police, as represented by Truscott. He shows policemen to be unashamedly violent and self-serving:

FAY: (*breaking down*) The British police force used to be run by men of integrity.
TRUSCOTT: That is a mistake which has been rectified...
(p255)

MCLEAVY: ... I've always been a law-abiding citizen. The police are for the protection of ordinary people.
TRUSCOTT: I don't know where you pick up these slogans, sir. You must read them on the hoardings.
(p274)

Orton's treatment of death

Orton's rage against the police is indeed purely negative. A positive criticism of the police would have involved some indication of how the police should behave rather than just a portrayal of how they should not. The character of Truscott is not balanced by that of a fine, upstanding officer presented as a positive rôle model. The most striking thing about *Loot*, however, is not the rage but the outrage. Orton flouts, or appears to flout, many sacred traditions of British life - faith in authority, respect for one's parents and reverence for the dead. His attitude to this last is linked to a 'positive creed' in which reverence is shifted away from the trappings of death and onto death itself. In *Plays and Players*, he explained: 'I have great reverence for death, but no particular feeling for the little dust of a corpse.' The corpse in *Loot* is merely an encumbrance. It is something which must be pulled from its coffin, dumped in a wardrobe and stripped to assist a group of thieves. Orton also said, in an interview with Giles Gordon: 'If you're absolutely practical - and I hope I am - a coffin is only a box. One calls it a coffin and once you've called it a coffin it immediately has all sorts of associations.' *Loot* strips away these associations. The coffin becomes, once more, only a box. It is a convenient hiding place for stolen money. Orton robs the corpse and the coffin of sanctity in order to return that sanctity to more important aspects of death. In the character of McLeavy, he presents a man who is apparently mourning his wife but is actually more interested in the rituals and accessories of death:

FAY: I sometimes think your father has a sentimental attachment to roses.
HAL: Do you know what his only comment was on my mother's death?
FAY: Something suitable, I'm sure.

...

HAL: He said he was glad she'd died at the right season for roses. He's been up half the night cataloguing the varieties on the crosses...
(p198-9)

McLeavy later describes the attempted funeral: 'Along the route perfect strangers had the courtesy to raise their hats. We got admiring glances for the flowers and sympathetic nods for me... The dignity of the event was unsurpassed.' (p237)

Despite his insistence on the solemnity of the occasion, he shows little respect for the memory of his late wife. His supposed mourning does not preclude some caustic comments about the deceased:

> HAL *and* DENNIS *enter with the coffin. It is charred, blackened and smoking.*
> FAY: Who'd think she'd be back so soon?
> MCLEAVY: She could never make up her mind in life. Death hasn't changed her.
> (p239)

> TRUSCOTT: (*to FAY*) Mrs McLeavy and I are perhaps the two people most closely involved in her death. I'd be interested to hear her on the subject.
> FAY: She accused her husband of murder.
> *Sensation.*
> MCLEAVY: Me? Are you sure she accused me?
> FAY: Yes.
> MCLEAVY: Complete extinction has done nothing to silence her slanderous tongue.
> (p252)

McLeavy insists that everything is in place for the funeral but never genuinely mourns his wife. Orton mocks McLeavy's hypocrisy and, in so doing, forces the audience to think about the true meaning of a loved one's death.

The impact of this message is often lost in productions. In a letter to the play's original producers, the Lord Chamberlain insisted that Mrs McLeavy must not be played by an actress but must be obviously a dummy. Even today, with no Lord Chamberlain to censor theatrical productions, the corpse is normally a vaguely anthropoid bundle of rags. Questions of reverence do not arise if the corpse is obviously a dummy. Since there is no taboo about tipping a dummy into a wardrobe or stripping a dummy, no taboo is questioned. For *Loot* to have its full effect, Mrs McLeavy must be played by an actress. It would not be a good part to play – second only to Yorick in *Hamlet* as a bum rôle – but it would raise questions about the status of a corpse. There is a chill attached to the spectacle of something that is obviously human in origin being treated as a means to an end rather than an end in itself. For the audience to enjoy this as comedy, it has to cultivate the insouciance of Hal who is told by Truscott: 'Your sense of detachment is terrifying, lad. Most people would at least flinch upon seeing their mother's eyes and teeth handed around like nuts at Christmas.' (p272) Once the audience has cultivated this insouciance, it can ask itself what is truly important concerning death.

Chapter Five
The minor plays

Orton bridged the gap between *Entertaining Mr Sloane* and *Loot* with his most bleakly realistic play.

The Good and Faithful Servant

On the day of his retirement, George Buchanan meets Edith, a woman with whom he had a brief affair when he was young. He learns for the first time of the twin boys that resulted from their liaison. They are both dead but one of them (nobody knows which) fathered a son, Ray, who now lives with Edith.

Buchanan has worked for his firm for fifty years and holds the record for long service. He also lost an arm in the course of his work. In the works canteen, public relations officer Mrs Vealfoy presents him with a clock and an electric toaster.

One of the younger employees, Debbie, seeks Mrs Vealfoy's advice because she is pregnant. Mrs Vealfoy promises to fix everything.

Buchanan arrives in Edith's front room. They have arranged to get married. Edith explains to Ray that Buchanan is his real grandfather. As she puts it: 'I was very silly, and Mr Buchanan behaved badly.' (p166) Ray is a dissolute young man without a job.

Buchanan plugs in his new toaster. There is a loud bang and a flash.

Debbie comes to Ray's room to tell him that she is pregnant with his child. He persuades her to stay the night. The next morning, Buchanan goes to Ray's room to convince him that what he really needs is a steady job. Buchanan finds Debbie hiding under the bed. Debbie admits her pregnancy to Edith and Buchanan. A shocked Buchanan says: 'Get away from me, Raymond. I'm disappointed in you.' Ray simply responds: 'But you did the same.' (p177)

Mrs Vealfoy persuades Ray that he must marry Debbie and embark on a career in the firm. She also persuades Buchanan to come along to her Bright Hours club for persons who are 'old, lonely and ex-members of the firm.' (p178) When he arrives at the club, he talks only to an old man who claims to know him but has just mistaken him for someone else. Buchanan realizes that nobody knows him, nobody remembers him. Back in Edith's room, he takes a hammer and smashes his retirement gifts. As Edith shows him the photographs of Debbie and Ray's wedding, Buchanan dies.

In *The Good and Faithful Servant*, Orton returns to a theme he explored in his first play, *Fred and Madge* - the futility of work. Fred and Madge realize in time that they have pointless jobs and go off to find a new life in India. Buchanan is four fifths dead before he realizes that his working life has been a waste of time. It is only towards the end of the play that he understands that he has spent fifty years working for a firm and has made not the slightest impact on anybody there. He has sedulously followed the rules and achieved nothing. The one time he broke the rules was when he seduced Edith. This youthful dalliance turns out to be his one source of joy in his last days. Despite this, he deplores Ray's activities with Debbie and pushes Ray towards a life of working tedium that will mirror his own. On Orton's terms, happiness comes from defiance of convention. Buchanan cannot see this until the very end of the play. To start with, Ray can.

Ray starts the play as one of the disreputable young men who appear throughout Orton's work. Like Sloane and Dennis, he makes a woman pregnant without taking the trouble to marry her first. Like Sloane and Hal, he has little interest in work and considers pleasure far more important than achievement. This attitude horrifies Buchanan:

RAY: I don't work.
BUCHANAN: Not work!? (*He stares, open-mouthed.*) What do you do then?
RAY: I enjoy myself.
BUCHANAN: That's a terrible thing to do...
(p167)

Buchanan has known only one way of life. It does not occur to him that there might be alternatives. He pushes Ray towards working in the old firm and sends him off to be won over by Mrs Vealfoy. She shares Buchanan's view and manœuvres Ray into taking a job with her breezy logic:

MRS VEALFOY: ... When you're married and have a wife and child you'll have to accept responsibility for them.
RAY: Yes.
MRS VEALFOY: You'll want a regular wage packet each week. (*With a smile, coup de grace.*) And so, you see, you must have a steady job. It's high time you began to consider a career.
(p182)

Ray succumbs to the pressure to conform. He joins the firm and sacrifices an interesting life for a secure one. Buchanan has already perpetuated the cycle of his own life when he realizes how pointless it's been. He does not see this until his visit to the Bright Hours club. He and an old man reflect sadly on what they have accomplished:

OLD MAN: I was almost mentioned in a well-known sporting periodical once.
BUCHANAN: I never got as far as that.
OLD MAN: I regard that as the high-spot of my life.
BUCHANAN: Yes. You would.
(p185)

A little later, Buchanan discovers that even this old man does not actually remember him:

BUCHANAN: But I worked here. I was on the main entrance. Are you sure you don't remember me?
OLD MAN: I'm sorry.
...

BUCHANAN: Nobody knows me. They've never seen me before.
(p189)

Buchanan's life has been his work. He has made no impression at work so no impression in life. He finally sees the pointlessness of it all. He goes back to Edith's house, takes a hammer and smashes to pieces the symbols of his fifty years' service. He dies just as Edith is saying: 'Raymond has quite reformed. Sees the error of his ways now. That's Debbie's influence. So you see even doing wrong as he did has its uses... It got him married. Settled. With a future before him.' (p191) The broken man lying dead beside her is a reminder of what that future is.

The Good and Faithful Servant sits uneasily in the Orton canon. The contempt for the established order is there as usual. What is missing is the gleeful defiance of it. Ray begins the play as a typically Ortonesque carefree, amoral young man. He finishes it in a very un-Ortonesque way by accepting that he has no choice but to join the establishment. Sloane, Hal, Dennis or Nick Beckett would have arranged to live comfortably off somebody else's work. Failing that, they would have charmed or blackmailed their way into some sinecure. Ray does neither of these things. He manfully sets out to support his family by the sweat of his brow. The result is that the play has a comforting predictability unusual in Orton. The message is that the young eventually accept that they must become like the old. The world of work will grind on as before and there is no choice but to grind on with it. There is none of Orton's characteristic anarchy.

The Erpingham Camp

This anarchy returns in *Loot* and in the play that followed it. *The Erpingham Camp* is the story of a small scale uprising against authority. The authority here is the management of a holiday camp. The crusaders are a group of disgruntled campers.

When the Entertainments Officer unexpectedly dies, holiday camp owner Mr Erpingham allows Chief Redcoat Riley to supervise the evening's amusements. When Riley is on stage, he asks if someone will dress up as Tarzan. One of the campers, Kenny, volunteers and is dressed in a leopard skin. Riley then calls on two ladies to take part in a screaming contest. Kenny's pregnant wife, Eileen, and her friend, Lou, come up on stage. Lou's husband, Ted, is persuaded onto the stage to do the can-can. During the contest, Eileen becomes hysterical and cannot stop screaming. Riley slaps her to shut her up. Kenny is incensed by this assault on his wife and attacks Riley. The fight develops into a pitch battle between campers and staff.

Erpingham steps in to restore order. Eileen hits him with a bottle. He decides to punish the campers by locking them out of their chalets and not providing any dinner. He locks the main gate so that nobody can leave. Ted and Lou appeal for calm among the campers but Kenny and Eileen incite them to riot. The campers break into Erpingham's office. Kenny attacks Erpingham who falls to his death through the floor. The shock of his dying stops the battle. Ted and Lou agree to support Kenny and Eileen if the matter should go before the police. Erpingham's body is brought in and the staff members file mournfully past.

The influence of Greek tragedy

John Lahr describes *The Erpingham Camp* as Orton's version of Euripides' *The Bacchae*. There are certainly similarities between the two plays. Each concerns a mob whipped into a frenzy and the individual who dies while trying to defy the mob will. The central character in *The Bacchae* is the god Dionysus. He arrives at Thebes to punish the king, Pentheus, for not honouring him in the city's prayers. He does this by driving the Theban women mad. Pentheus is finally torn to pieces by a gang of ecstatic women led by his own mother.

Erpingham, king in his own little city, is the character equivalent to Pentheus. Pentheus believes he can end the women's revels by force: 'Once I have them secure in iron chains I shall soon put a stop to this outrageous Bacchism.' Erpingham believes he can quell the uprising if he remains strongly resolute:

KENNY: ... It's every man's right to protect his wife.
...
ERPINGHAM: You're talking nonsense. You have no rights. You have certain privileges which can be withdrawn. I am withdrawing them.
...
KENNY: We want food. We demand bread. We expect shelter!
    ERPINGHAM *is made angry by the tone of* KENNY's
    voice.
ERPINGHAM: You have damaged my property, poured scorn upon my staff and insulted me. You've cast my hospitality in my face. And yet, the bitter taste of ingratitude not dry upon my lips, you come to me with your arrogant demands. No. You must be taught a lesson. There will be no food tonight. I shall not give way. You can sleep in the open. The chalet area is closed until further notice.
(p307)

Both Erpingham and Pentheus suffer as a result of denying their people certain human rights. Erpingham denies Kenny the right to defend his wife. He then denies the campers food and shelter. Pentheus denies the Theban women the right to worship their god.

    The bulk of Pentheus' outrage is directed not at the Dionysiac women but at Dionysus himself. The focus for Erpingham's rage is Kenny, who is the character most similar to Dionysus. Although it is Riley who sets the revels in train by encouraging such Bacchic excesses as dancing the can-can and screaming, it is Kenny who stirs up revolutionary fervour amongst the campers: '...in the life of every one of us, there comes a time when he must choose – whether to be treated in the manner of the bad old days. Or whether to take by force those common human rights which should be denied no man... A place to sleep, food for our kids, and respect. That's all we ask. Is it too much?' (p309) Orton emphasizes Kenny's Dionysian rôle by dressing him appropriately. Dionysus traditionally rides a leopard-drawn chariot. In order to play Tarzan, Kenny has been dressed in a leopard skin which he wears for the rest of the play.

It is also significant that, of all Orton's plays, *The Erpingham Camp* is the one which makes the most use of music. In *The Birth of Tragedy*, Nietzsche points out that the experience of a Greek tragedy, as originally performed, was essentially a musical one. People today can have little inkling of the full original impact of one of these tragedies as the music has not survived. For Nietzsche, music is the quintessentially Dionysian art form. The crowd reaches a state of Dionysian ecstasy by being collectively caught up in the music. In his most Dionysian play, Orton includes the stage direction that 'The Holy City' be played while Erpingham is dreaming of the holiday camp empire he will build. 'Zadok the Priest and Nathan the Prophet Anointed Solomon King' plays while Riley is being ordained as entertainments officer. The Redcoats sing and dance a medley of songs before the entertainment begins. Riley opens the show with a rendition of 'My Irish Song of Songs.' 'La Marseillaise' plays as the campers go on the rampage and the staff file past Erpingham's body to the strains of 'The Last Post.' These snatches are unlikely to induce Dionysian ecstasy in *The Erpingham Camp*'s audience but they heighten the similarity between Orton's comedy and Greek tragedy.

The Erpingham Camp is not the only play in which Orton shows evidence of the classical education he acquired through Halliwell. He uses the same Dionysian image in *What the Butler Saw*. When Sergeant Match is deprived of his uniform, he is wrapped in a leopard skin dress. He is wearing this when he performs his godlike rôle at the end of the play. He is the *deus ex machina* who descends from the sky to restore order. He does this by returning the stone figure of Churchill's penis to its rightful place. Everything has gone wrong for Geraldine while she has had this symbol of the nation's heritage in her possession. This is reminiscent of Ajax, plagued with misfortune while he has Hector's sword, another potent symbol of national heritage. Also in *What the Butler Saw*, Nick discovers, in true Oedipus fashion, that he has inadvertently slept with his mother. In *Entertaining*

Mr Sloane, Sloane may have committed the Oedipal sin by sleeping with Kath as there are hints she may be his mother. Kemp refuses to talk to Ed, his son, a situation that Orton admitted to borrowing from *Oedipus at Colonus*. And in *Funeral Games*, McCorquodale condemns Bishop Goodheart's lascivious activities with the words: 'Oh, the bacchic hound!' (p332)

Funeral Games

Funeral Games is the last play Orton wrote before his masterpiece, *What the Butler Saw*. Considering what was to come straight after it, *Funeral Games* is surprisingly weak.

Pringle, the leader of an eccentric religious group, summons a private detective when he receives an anonymous letter accusing his wife, Tessa, of adultery. The letter gives the address at which her indiscretions allegedly take place. The detective, Caulfield, goes to investigate. He finds that Tessa is merely looking after an elderly defrocked priest, McCorquodale – a man physically incapable of adultery. Tessa was a friend of McCorquodale's late wife, Val. Caulfield discovers that McCorquodale killed his wife after he caught her cavorting with a man calling himself Bishop Goodheart. She is buried under a ton of coal in McCorquodale's cellar. Pringle is not impressed by Caulfield's report of Tessa's innocence. He has had a religious experience in which he was told that 'Thou shalt not suffer an adulteress to live.' He arms himself and goes to McCorquodale's to shoot Tessa. He is stopped when Caulfield smashes a bottle over his head. When he revives, he is distraught to find Tessa still alive. He has vowed to his flock that he would kill her and now fears ridicule. Tessa suggests that he just pretend to have killed her. Pringle agrees and anticipates that the headline: 'Vengeance is Mine says No Nonsense Parson' will increase his congregation a thousandfold. Tessa will stay with McCorquodale and pose as his wife.

Pringle becomes a celebrity. 'When rumour got around that I'd murdered my wife, my phone never stopped ringing.' (p343) However, he receives a letter from a crime reporter called Paterson. Paterson accuses Pringle of being a fraud and demands proof that he really has murdered his wife. Caulfield tells Pringle that he does not need a complete dead body: part of one will do. Caulfield goes down to McCorquodale's cellar to cut off the late Mrs McCorquodale's head. It won't come off so he cuts off one of her hands instead. He puts the severed hand into a cake tin and takes Val's watch for himself. Tessa recognizes the watch. This, coupled with her discovery of the hand in the tin, determines her to go to the police and tell all. Caulfield stops her by tying her up.

Pringle returns from a meeting with Paterson, at which he showed Paterson the hand in the cake tin. Caulfield tells Pringle that he'll have to murder his wife or she'll accuse him of not being a murderer. McCorquodale drags in a trunk that will serve as Tessa's coffin. She frees herself from her bonds with a circumcising knife she finds in the trunk. Pringle and Caulfield burst in just as she's escaping. McCorquodale identifies Pringle as the lecherous Bishop Goodheart. McCorquodale threatens to expose Pringle as a fraud. Pringle tells Tessa that she can't establish McCorquodale's guilt without establishing Pringle's innocence. Caulfield suggests that Pringle identify Mrs McCorquodale as his deceased wife. Caulfield takes the hand from the cake tin. He discovers that the real hand has been replaced by a fake one. Paterson has stolen the real hand and taken it to the police. The play ends with the arrival of the police and the arrest of all the characters.

Funeral Games is weak for several reasons. One is that it features dialogue that would have been rejected as too corny by the *Carry On* team:

CAULFIELD: (*to* MCCORQUODALE) I couldn't get her head off. It must be glued on.
MCCORQUODALE: She was always a headstrong woman.
(p347-8)

Substandard comedy would be less of a problem if the play weren't so unsatisfying as drama. In *What the Butler Saw*, the different strands of the plot combine at the end to form a brilliant climax. In *Funeral Games*, the different strands become impossibly tangled. McCorquodale attacks Pringle for having seduced his wife. They start a fight which is soon abandoned when Caulfield tries to stop Tessa from going to the police by shooting her in the face. That idea is also abandoned when Caulfield discovers that the gun is empty. He and Pringle then attempt to convince her that Val deserved everything she got:

MCCORQUODALE: He was making a breach in the seventh command-ment and my wife. (*To* PRINGLE) That's foul churching, Bishop.
TESSA: (*to* PRINGLE) How long had it been going on?
PRINGLE: The spirit of the Brotherhood entered Valerie about a year prior to her death.
TESSA: How could she sink so low?
CAULFIELD: He got in under her guard. It's a familiar technique of dance-hall seducers.
TESSA: She was so well brought up.
CAULFIELD: It's the well brought up ones that go first. As every small-time Romeo knows.
TESSA: Stealing my husband and concealing the fact that she had one of her own. It's scandalous behaviour.
(p357-8)

This unconvincing dialogue somehow convinces Tessa. She decides not to go to the police giving her reason as: 'She tempted the Lord. It would be blasphemous to raise a hand in her defence.' (p358)
Caulfield then threatens to blackmail Pringle unless he is employed by the church.

The characters open up all these lines of development but not one of them leads the play to a satisfactory conclusion. In *Entertaining Mr Sloane*, *Loot* and *What the Butler Saw*, the characters arrive at a compromise which is amoral but which allows their interests to be satisfied. Orton does not manage to get the characters of *Funeral Games* to this point. He falls back on the hackneyed ending of the police arriving to arrest everybody. On Orton's terms, this is a definite regression from the final version of *Loot*. In earlier versions, Truscott arrested Hal, Dennis and Fay so he could keep the money for himself. This ending offers the audience partial reassurance that justice still prevails. The policeman may be corrupt but at least the criminals are punished. By the final version, there is no such comfort. Truscott, Hal, Dennis and Fay share the ill-gotten gains between them and send the innocent McLeavy to prison. The key feature of Orton's drama is that the individual replaces society's rules with his own. This feature is brought out in the final draft of *Loot*. It is surprising that he gave the later *Funeral Games* such a conventional ending: an investigative journalist uncovers wrongdoings and has the miscreants arrested. And when the police officers do arrive, they are, bizarrely for Orton, only interested in doing their duty. They don't even suggest bribery.

The triteness of the ending, coupled with the stale motif of the man resolved to punish adultery turning out to be an adulterer himself, make this the least of the mature Orton's plays. It does not work as either comedy or drama.

Up Against It

Up Against It was Orton's first real foray into writing for the big screen. In 1964, Lindsay Anderson asked him to work on a modern film version of *The Bacchae*. The idea never got beyond the treatment stage and eventually formed the basis of *The Erpingham Camp*. Orton always had suspicions that the *Up Against It* project would go the same way and so was determined to enjoy himself while he wrote it.

Two young men, Ian McTurk and Christopher Low, are expelled from the city of their birth by Father Brodie, police chief Connie and the mayor. Low is accused of blowing up the city's war memorial, McTurk of seducing Brodie's niece, Rowena. McTurk leaves behind the broken-hearted Patricia Drumgoole, whom he loved and left. He can think only of the lovely Rowena. The two men set out through a dark forest to begin a new life. They part when Low goes off to answer a cry of distress. McTurk realizes that no good can come of helping people. Low finds a fat man at the bottom of a hole and pulls him out. The fat man then attacks him and is about to fling him into the hole when Bernard Coates arrives. Coates hurls the fat man back into the hole. Coates offers to take Low to a party but Low loses him among the trees. Low finds his way to a large house which turns out to belong to Coates. Coates is agitated about the results of a recent election: Lillian Corbett has been elected the country's first woman prime minister. Coates leaves Low to read about her in the newspaper. Connie appears and gives Low a room. In the rose garden outside the house, McTurk has a passionate reunion with Rowena. Rowena is supposed to be stopping off at Coates' house on her way to join a convent. Meanwhile, Connie is roughly seducing Low in a luxuriously appointed bedroom.

McTurk is having breakfast in the kitchen. Miss Drumgoole, who says she's accompanying Rowena to the convent, tells him that Rowena has given instructions that he must leave the house as soon as he's eaten. Rowena is to marry Coates. McTurk leaves the house and runs into a group of political activists led by Jack Ramsay. Without Rowena, McTurk has nothing to live for, so he joins the organization. Among its members are Low, Miss Drumgoole and the ex-mayor of the town where McTurk was born. The group's aim is to assassinate Mrs Corbett at a conference in the Albert Hall. Unfortunately, only women are allowed into the conference, so McTurk, Low and Ramsay attend in drag. They shoot the prime minister. They then disrupt her funeral with anti-government speeches. Riots break out when the police arrive.

Connie is made the new premier. She knows that McTurk was responsible for the assassination so she drafts in Rowena to help in his capture. He is on the frontline, battling against the police when he receives a note from Rowena. She lures him into a garden where he is seized by policewomen. He is taken to prison where the governor is none other than Bernard Coates. Coates tells McTurk that he cannot appeal against his sentence as only tall people have the right of appeal and he is too short. Coates promises to put him in a better cell and puts him in one that's much worse. When he has been in prison for ten years, Ramsay tunnels in to rescue him. They escape into the sewer and are carried out to sea. They are picked up by a yacht, on which the cabin boy is one Christopher Low. Also on board are Miss Drumgoole, Coates and his wife, Rowena. She admits to McTurk that she only married Coates for his money. McTurk attempts unsuccessfully to seduce her. Coates responds by throwing him – along with Low and Ramsay – off the ship. As they are tossed about in a lifeboat, they come across Miss Drumgoole who was washed overboard last night. She climbs onto the boat, which sinks beneath the extra weight.

McTurk drags himself onto a beach. A group of nurses take him to hospital. There he meets Connie, who enlists him to fight in her regiment against the rebels. At the recruitment centre, he meets Low and Ramsay who have decided to help in crushing the rebellion they started. The three of them are at an army camp when Miss Drumgoole arrives to entertain the troops with her cabaret act. McTurk still refuses to marry her, pleading a broken heart as an excuse. All four decide to desert and rejoin the rebels. As they are leaving in Miss Drumgoole's van, they are stopped by a sentry – the ex-mayor – who joins the desertion. The van is destroyed by a landmine.

McTurk finds himself back in hospital. Low and Ramsay arrive at visiting time and tell him they've joined the rebels. Coates is their commanding officer. He and Rowena have parted. The next day, McTurk arrives at the rebel camp. Coates hears that the enemy is only a mile away and orders a retreat. McTurk jumps into a lorry. It shoots forward and crashes into an ambulance. A chaotic chain reaction is triggered. Lorries and ambulances explode. Government troops led by Connie attack with guns and grenades. The ground beneath them caves in and they all crash into the hole. Father Brodie arrives with a pack of nuns and choir boys to sing a hymn.

The government troops have won. McTurk, Low and Ramsay are hailed as heroes for setting in train the events which resulted in the rebels' defeat. Peace brings no joy to McTurk. Rowena and Coates are back together. McTurk can never marry the woman he loves. Low is set to marry Connie but breaks it off when he hears her philistine views about the role of men in society. The three young men meet Miss Drumgoole. They all decide that they want to marry her. She agrees that they should all marry and live as a happy quartet. Father Brodie presides at the wedding. The screenplay ends with a delighted Patricia Drumgoole disappearing under the bedclothes with her husbands.

Orton rewrote the screenplay for Oscar Lewenstein after it was rejected by the Beatles' office. He said of the revised version: 'I've turned the four Beatles into three young men. It's a much better script without the weight of stars hanging on it.' It nonetheless betrays its origins as a star vehicle. The picaresque form in drama lends itself to a large number of character actors rather than to three or four stars. In the traditional picaresque, the main character goes from place to place meeting different interesting people. *In Up Against It*, McTurk goes from place to place meeting the same interesting people. By having Low, Ramsay, Coates and Miss Drumgoole appear in many places throughout McTurk's odyssey, Orton is able to use the picaresque form while writing five large parts for leading performers to play.

The picaresque form suits the grand ambitions of the screenplay. Freed from the confines of space and budget imposed by theatre or television, Orton had no need to restrict his characters to one or two rooms. The freedom went to his head and he gave his action large scale settings - a forest, a stately home, a conference hall full of delegates, a street riot, a prison, a luxury yacht, a battlefield. The relentless rushing from one arena to another is dizzying on the page. It would be still more dizzying on the screen.

Orton's portrayal of women

Up Against It presents a Britain ruled by women. Orton gave the country a female prime minister twelve years before the electorate did. Lillian Corbett, however, is no Margaret Thatcher. She and her all-female cabinet have no interest in affairs of state and spend their time discussing clothes, make-up and decor. They behave more like drag queens than like real women. Mrs Corbett's speech at the conference is not a classic piece of political rhetoric:

PRIME MINISTER: This is my first report as Prime Minister and I'd like to commence by paying to the ladies of the cabinet an immediate tribute. How they manage to run the country and remain so attractive I do not know. ...Well, dears, we've just had the most heavenly cabinet meeting!
    MRS O'SCULLION *struggles to her feet. Her face is flushed. Her lip trembles.*
MRS O'SCULLION: Oh, Lillian! And I wasn't there! How could you!
...
    She stamps her foot. Bursts into tears. Dabbing her eyes she runs from the platform. The PRIME MINISTER *sighs.*
PRIME MINISTER: Georgina gets so excited by the smallest things. I sometimes wonder whether it was altogether wise to give her the Foreign Office. (*She flicks ash from her cigarette end.*) We had the meeting at Molly's house. And we've come to a decision that is sure to have far-reaching consequences... We're having the House of Commons redecorated in Chinese white lacquer and natural oak woodwork!
(p29)

This idea that women are over-emotional, have no head for business and concern themselves solely with frippery echoes Ed's attitude in *Entertaining Mr Sloane*: 'I live in a world of top decisions. We've no time for ladies.' (p90) It is not clear if this was Orton's own attitude. In life, his attitude to women was ambivalent. Although definitely homosexual rather than bisexual, he was not blind to feminine charms. In his diary, he writes about a morning spent with 'the beautiful

German (or Danish) Vipsil':

> ... for a morning's walk around the town, I possessed the most beautiful and desirable girl in Tangier. I was curiously excited by this fact... We swam. I dived from the top board... - to impress Vipsil - why I should want to impress her is impossible to imagine. (19 May 1967)

He enjoyed being with Vipsil mainly because of the envious looks he attracted from other men. At times, however, he enjoyed the company of women for their intrinsic qualities. Sheila Ballantine, who played Fay in the first London production of *Loot*, recalls: 'He used to pick me up and whirl me around the dressing-room. You just had to love him. Everybody did. Joe made life very exciting. He became very important in my life. We were going to go on vacations. We were going to have adventures.' At other times, however, he expressed great approval for areas of Tangier that were entirely free from women.

In his work, the interesting characters tend to be the young men – Wilson, Sloane, Hal and Dennis, Caulfield, McTurk, Nick. The women are often just means to an end. Joyce in *The Ruffian on the Stair* is there simply to be seduced, not for any qualities she has, but so that two men can settle a score. Geraldine in *What the Butler Saw* is also there to be seduced by Dr Prentice, thus setting in train the farcical events. After that, she becomes the blank canvas onto which Dr Rance projects his psychiatric theories. Kath is a feeble character for most of *Entertaining Mr Sloane*. She can assert herself only with a frail old man and is dominated by Sloane and Ed. Only at the end does she stand up for herself. She is, throughout, an unpleasant character – repulsive in her habits, a seducer of young men, pathetically yearning for attention and affection.

Fay in *Loot* is Orton's most interesting female character. The difference between her and Orton's other women is that she is active while the others are passive. She does things. The others have things done to them. She murders Mrs McLeavy and then assists in the disposal of her body. She manœuvres McLeavy into proposing to her. She suggests to Truscott that McLeavy might accidentally die in his prison cell. She finally agrees to marry Dennis and tells Hal that he must move out – thus splitting up one partnership so that she and Dennis can form a new one. She appears to be a manipulative bitch but that is only because she is as ruthlessly pragmatic as the male characters. Just as Hal will hide stolen money in his mother's coffin if there is nowhere else available, so Fay will marry McLeavy or Dennis, whoever has more money. She is no more immoral than Hal, Dennis or Truscott. Orton is not being misogynistic in his portrayal of her – quite the contrary. He is showing his audience that a woman can be just as strong-willed and resourceful as a man in achieving her ends. Fay is a one-off in this respect. In the play that followed *Loot* - *The Erpingham Camp* – Eileen is there to be assaulted, thus sparking revolution, Lou is there to agree with whatever her husband says and Jessie Mason, the accordionist, is there to be the butt of holiday camp humour about men wanting to get their fingers on her squeeze-box.

*

Orton's minor plays have their flaws but show the development of his talents. He had a natural gift for dialogue. He had to work hard at training this dialogue to expound plots and at marrying it with action.

In his last play, the dialogue is fast, epigrammatical and very funny. He moves the characters around the stage like a speed chess champion. The plot is tightly-constructed and moves at a frenetic pace towards a thrilling conclusion. All the promise of his earlier plays is fulfilled.

What the Butler Saw is the brilliant justification of all his efforts.

Chapter Six
What the Butler Saw

The action of *What the Butler Saw* takes place in the consulting room of Dr Prentice's psychiatric clinic. Dr Prentice attempts to seduce his prospective secretary, Geraldine Barclay, by asking her to undress. Geraldine is distressed as her adoptive mother has just been killed in an explosion which also damaged a statue of Winston Churchill. Dr Prentice has Geraldine naked behind the curtains of his couch, when his wife unexpectedly returns.

Mrs Prentice is being blackmailed by hotel page Nicholas Beckett. He has a series of compromising photographs of her, taken while he was seducing her. She takes Geraldine's dress to replace the one stolen by Nick.

Dr Rance, a government official, arrives to inspect the clinic. He finds the naked Geraldine behind the curtains. Dr Prentice passes her off as a patient who has taken his secretary's name as her 'nom-de-folie.' Dr Rance certifies her insane, convinced that she behaves in this way because she has been sexually assaulted by her father. Geraldine is believed to be a patient so Dr Prentice has to account for the disappearance of his secretary. He does this by asking Nick to put on a dress and to pretend to be Geraldine.

Meanwhile, a policeman, Sergeant Match, has arrived to question Nick about his sex crimes. Match also believes that Geraldine can help him trace the missing part of the statue of Winston Churchill. Geraldine herself has recovered her underwear and is running round the clinic wearing nothing else. She eventually covers herself up by putting on Nick's discarded page uniform.

Act Two opens with Match questioning Geraldine, believing her to be Nick. She accuses Dr Prentice of trying to seduce her. As the others believe her to be a boy, this casts doubt on Dr Prentice's sexuality. Mrs Prentice says that Geraldine is not the boy who seduced her. Nick is pretending to be Geraldine so Dr Prentice now has to account for Nick's disappearance. Nick suggests that if he borrows Match's uniform, he can arrest himself and be taken out of the picture. Dr Prentice persuades Match to undress and drugs him. Dr Prentice covers Match with Mrs Prentice's dress and drags him into the garden to sleep it off. Dr Rance and Mrs Prentice see him, apparently dragging a dead woman, and suspect him of having murdered Geraldine. Dr Prentice denies the charge of murder. He says that Geraldine is hiding because Mrs Prentice is wearing Geraldine's dress. He finally confesses the attempted seduction to his wife. Mrs Prentice does not believe him as she is now convinced that he is homosexual.

Nick enters, dressed as a policeman. He announces that he is Nick's brother and has arrested Nick. When Mrs Prentice tells him that her husband has killed Geraldine, Nick drops the disguise as he does not want to assist a murderer. Dr Rance and Mrs Prentice persuade Nick to put Dr Prentice into a straitjacket. Dr Prentice resists and tells Nick and Geraldine to put their own clothes back on.

Dr Rance and Mrs Prentice have armed themselves. Dr Rance sees Geraldine and, triumphant at having recaptured his patient, uses the gun to force her into a straitjacket. Dr Rance and Dr Prentice confront each other and threaten to certify each other. Dr Prentice and Geraldine explain to Dr Rance why she disappeared. Dr Rance cannot accept that Geraldine is not mad and that his diagnosis of her as a victim of incest appears incorrect. He is also disappointed that Dr Prentice is not a murderer as that story would have made a best-selling book.

Geraldine announces that she has lost her lucky elephant charm. Dr Rance finds it. Nick has an identical charm. The two charms can be put together to form a single brooch. Mrs Prentice reveals that she was given the brooch by a man who raped her many years ago. As a result of the rape, she conceived twins whom she was forced to abandon. She gave each twin one half of the brooch. Dr Prentice admits that it was he who raped Mrs Prentice.

Dr Rance's diagnosis is proved correct: Geraldine was indeed assaulted by her father when Dr Prentice tried to seduce her. He can now write his book about the case in good faith. Mrs Prentice reminds him that as Nick is her son, she has also been the victim of an incestuous assault. Dr Rance is overjoyed as 'Double incest is even more likely to produce a best-seller than murder...' (p446)

Sergeant Match descends through the skylight, demanding that someone produce the missing part of the statue of Winston Churchill. It turns out that the bronze cast of the great man's penis was embedded in the late Mrs Barclay's body and is in the box given to Geraldine by the undertaker. The box is discovered and Match holds aloft 'the nation's heritage.' The play ends with Dr Rance advising: 'Let us put our clothes on and face the world.' (p448)

The treatment of psychiatry

Martin Esslin says of *What the Butler Saw*: '... there is not even a hint of a genuine critique of psychiatry or psychoanalysis in the play.' This is demonstrably false. Orton's critique of psychiatry is that it is essentially non-empirical. Dr Rance has his theory about Geraldine's condition. Nothing that anyone says or does will be allowed to disprove this theory.

Orton's portrayal of psychiatry has echoes of Karl Popper's remarks in *Conjectures and Refutations*. Popper uses the methods of psychiatrists to show that psychiatry is not part of science. For Popper, a theory is scientific only if some conceivable experimental evidence could prove it wrong. No evidence is allowed to prove a psychiatric theory wrong. In his opening chapter, Popper writes:

> I found that those of my friends who were admirers of Marx, Freud and Adler, were impressed by a number of points common to these theories, and especially by their apparent *explanatory power*. These theories appeared to be able to explain practically everything that happened within the fields to which they referred... Once your eyes were thus opened you saw confirming instances everywhere: the world was full of *verifications* of the theory. Whatever happened always confirmed it. (Popper's italics.)

This is the attitude taken by Dr Rance. He has come up with the theory that Geraldine was assaulted by her father. Even Geraldine's denials can be used to confirm this theory:

RANCE: ...(*To* GERALDINE) Who was the first man in your life?
GERALDINE: My father.
RANCE: Did he assault you?
GERALDINE: No!
RANCE: (*to* DR PRENTICE) She may mean 'Yes' when she says 'No.' It's elementary feminine psychology.
(p382)

A little later, Dr Rance asks Geraldine again:

RANCE: ... Were you molested by your father?
GERALDINE: (*with a scream of horror*) No, no, no!
    DR RANCE *straightens up and faces* DR PRENTICE.
RANCE: The vehemence of her denials is proof positive of guilt. It's a text-book case! A man beyond innocence, a girl aching for experience. The beauty, confusion and urgency of their passion driving them on. They embark on a reckless love-affair. He finds it difficult to reconcile his guilty secret with his spiritual convictions. It preys on his mind. Sexual activity ceases. She, who basked in his love, feels anxiety at its loss. She seeks advice from her priest. The Church, true to Her ancient traditions, counsels chastity. The result - madness.
PRENTICE: It's a fascinating theory, sir, and cleverly put together. Does it tie in with known facts?
RANCE: That need not cause us undue anxiety. Civilizations have been founded and maintained on theories which refused to obey facts. As far as I'm concerned this child was unnaturally assaulted by her own father. I shall base my future actions upon that assumption.
(p382-3)

Geraldine is not the only one to fall victim to Rance's unshakeable faith in his own theories. Throughout the play, he makes snap judgments about people and then defends these judgments against any contrary evidence:

PRENTICE: Miss Barclay is no more ill than I am.
RANCE: But your condition is worse than hers.
PRENTICE: I can't accept that.
RANCE: No madman ever accepts madness. Only the sane do that.
(p415)

PRENTICE: Your interpretation of my behaviour is misplaced and erroneous. If anyone borders on lunacy it's you yourself!
RANCE: Bearing in mind your abnormality that is a normal reaction. The sane appear as strange to the mad as the mad to the sane.
(p418)

When Mrs Prentice sees the sergeant undressing and then sees Nick changing into the sergeant's uniform, she unwisely appeals to Dr Rance:

MRS PRENTICE: ... You must help me, doctor! I keep seeing naked men.
RANCE: (*pause*) When did these delusions start?
MRS PRENTICE: They're not delusions. They're real.
RANCE: (*with a bray of laughter*) Everyone who suffers from hallucinations imagines they are real. When did you last think you saw a naked man?
MRS PRENTICE: Just now. He was nude except for a policeman's helmet.
RANCE: (*drily*) It's not difficult to guess what's on your mind, my dear. Are you having marital troubles?
(p422-3)

Flouting the conventions of farce

Orton uses Rance's methods to increase his characters' sense of dislocation and loss of identity. Here, Orton moves away from the cosy conventions of traditional farce, in which order is restored when the characters stop dissembling and finally tell each other the truth. In *What the Butler Saw*, the truth has no power against Dr Rance. He interprets all evidence in his own way. The truth for him is whatever he needs to support his theories. Rance believes Geraldine to be insane. Nothing she can do can stop her from suffering the humiliation of having her head shaved and of being drugged, straitjacketed and confined to a padded cell. When she is dressed as a boy, her protests that she is a girl carry no weight with Dr Rance. As he is convinced that she is a boy who has been abused by Dr Prentice, he merely assumes that the boy is adopting a female identity to assuage the guilt brought on by homosexual activity. Geraldine is reduced to flinging herself into Rance's arms and crying: 'Undress me then, doctor! Do whatever you like only prove that I'm a girl.' Even this does not help her cause. Dr Rance takes it as another sign of madness and says: 'If he's going to carry on like this he'll have to be strapped down.' (p414)

Dr Prentice is a more traditional farce character. He is convinced that if he is clever enough, he can conceal his misdemeanours from those around him. In Act One, Geraldine tells him: 'We must tell the truth!' He dismisses the ludicrous suggestion with a cry of: 'That's a thoroughly defeatist attitude.' (p400) By Act Two, however, the situation has developed to a point where he must reluctantly resort to the truth. When he is suspected of murder, it no longer seems important to conceal his attempted seduction:

PRENTICE: (*swallowing whisky*) Miss Barclay isn't dead!
MRS PRENTICE: Produce her then and your difficulties will be over.
PRENTICE: I can't.
MRS PRENTICE: Why not?
PRENTICE: You're wearing her dress. (*With a shrug of resignation.*) You surprised me this morning making an ill-timed attempt to seduce her. (p430)

Now that Prentice has dropped the pretence that started the whole chain of events, he should, according to the conventions of farce, be on his way to a resolution of the chaos. The truth, however, does not help him. He is a conventional farce figure trapped in an unconventional farce. Mrs Prentice merely 'smiles a smile of quiet disbelief' and responds: 'If we're to save our marriage, my dear, you must admit that you prefer boys to women.' Her next words reveal the origin of the way of thinking she has accepted: 'Dr Rance has explained the reasons for your aberration.' As Dr Rance has established his own criterion for what will be accepted as true, the only possible resolution is the one which will satisfy him. He must be proved right before the characters can return to anything like normality.

Orton reaches this resolution by presenting the audience with what looks, at first sight, to be a conventional happy ending. Nick is revealed as Geraldine's brother. Dr and Mrs Prentice are their parents. The family members are reunited and embrace each other on stage. In many plays, this would be the point to bring down the curtain and take a bow. Orton, however, does not allow his audience the luxury of forgetting the implications of these revelations. Dr Rance immediately reminds the audience that the happy family enjoying the group hug is a highly dysfunctional one:

RANCE: (*to* PRENTICE *wild with delight*) If you are this child's father my book can be written in good faith - she is the victim of an incestuous assault!
MRS PRENTICE: And so am I, doctor! My son has a collection of indecent photographs which prove beyond doubt that he made free with me...
RANCE: Oh, what joy this discovery brings me!
(p446)

Everything now fits into the pattern prescribed by Dr Rance. Only now can the chaos be resolved.

Similarities with Oscar Wilde

In 1966, Orton said: 'I'd like to write a play as good as *The Importance of Being Earnest*.' There are similarities between Wilde's play and *What the Butler Saw*. Each play involves characters pretending to be other people. Each is resolved with the discovery that the main characters are part of the same family. Each derives much of its humour from dialogue that follows a heartless logic. For example:

ALGERNON: ... poor Bunbury is a dreadful invalid.
LADY BRACKNELL: Well, I must say, Algernon, that I think it is high time that Mr Bunbury made up his mind whether he was going to live or die. This shilly-shallying with the question is absurd. Nor do I in any way approve of the modern sympathy with invalids. I consider it morbid. Illness of any kind is hardly a thing to be encouraged in others.
(*The Importance of Being Earnest*, Act One)

The comedy here derives from Lady Bracknell's insistence on applying such values as decisiveness and the encouragement of the good in areas where taste demands that they are waived – illness and death. She employs a simple logic which states that if a principle is good, it should be applied in all areas. In following this logic, she shows no sympathy whatever for the ailing Mr Bunbury.

In *What the Butler Saw*, this heartless logic is taken to new levels. There is an autism about Dr Rance and Dr Prentice which prevents them from caring about the people around them. Their responses to others' misfortune do not accord with social conventions. They do not, however, speak in Pinteresque non sequiturs. Their remarks are unexpected but nevertheless follow logically from what has gone before:

GERALDINE: ... I was brought up by a Mrs Barclay. She died recently.
PRENTICE: From what cause?
GERALDINE: An explosion, due to a faulty gas-main, killed her outright and took the roof off the house.
PRENTICE: Have you applied for compensation?
(p365)

This is a reasonable question to ask in the light of what Geraldine has just said. But convention and good taste dictate that Dr Prentice's first words should be of sympathy at Geraldine's bereavement. Neither Dr Prentice nor Dr Rance shows any sympathy for Mrs Prentice when she tells them of the assault made on her:

MRS PRENTICE: ... I found a page-boy who enticed me into the cupboard and then made an indecent suggestion. When I repulsed him he attempted to rape me. I fought him off but not before he'd stolen my handbag and several articles of clothing.
PRENTICE: It doesn't sound the kind of behaviour one expects at a four-star hotel.
(p374)

RANCE: What was the object of this assault?
MRS PRENTICE: The youth wanted to rape me.
RANCE: He didn't succeed?
MRS PRENTICE: No.
RANCE: (*shaking his head*) The service in these hotels is dreadful.
(p390)

What the Butler Saw is a more exhilarating play than *The Importance of Being Earnest*. In Wilde's play, the characters are motivated merely by boredom or curiosity. Jack has invented a black sheep brother Ernest so that he has an excuse to go to town whenever he is bored of the country. Algernon pretends to be Ernest merely because he is intrigued by Jack's ward, Cecily. Orton's characters are motivated by real needs. It is no idle whim that makes Geraldine dress up in Nick's uniform. Without clothes of some sort, she cannot leave the clinic. If she does not escape, she will be confined to a padded cell. Nick must pretend to be a policeman and pretend to arrest himself or he really will be arrested by the real policeman. It is this necessity that causes *What the Butler Saw* to move at such a frenetic pace. The urgency is reflected in the dialogue. Wilde's characters have the leisure to snipe at each other elegantly over tea. Orton's characters fire lines at each other as they rush from one crisis to the next.

In *The Importance of Being Earnest*, there are longueurs and patches of pedestrian dialogue between the famous pieces of wit. In *What the Butler Saw*, the good lines pile up on top of each other. If anything, there are too many good lines. In any production of the play, not all the lines can get the laughs they deserve. Another line has been delivered before the audience has finished laughing at the last one. For example:

MRS PRENTICE: (*quietly*) I hardly ever have sexual intercourse.
PRENTICE: You were born with your legs apart. They'll send you to the grave in a Y-shaped coffin.
MRS PRENTICE: My trouble stems from your inadequacy as a lover! It's embarrassing. You must've learned your technique from a Christmas cracker. (*Her mouth twists into a sneer.*) Rejuvenation pills have no effect on you.
PRENTICE: (*stuffily*) I never take pills.
MRS PRENTICE: You take them all the time during our love-making. The deafening sound of your chewing is the reason for my never having an orgasm.
...
PRENTICE: How dare you say that! Your book on the climax in the female is largely autobiographical. (*Pause. He stares.*) Or have you been masquerading as a sexually responsive woman?
MRS PRENTICE: My uterine contractions have been bogus for some time!
...
PRENTICE: (*looking after her*) What a discovery! Married to the mistress of the fraudulent climax.
(p371-2)

Such dialogue needs to be delivered at a rapid pace to have its full effect. But where does the audience laugh? Dr Prentice delivers the punchline: 'They'll send you to the grave in a Y-shaped coffin.' Mrs Prentice responds with another punchline: 'You must've learned your technique from a Christmas cracker.'

This is not a major criticism of the play. After all, if one has good lines to burn, it is no great calamity if some of them get burnt.

Orton's play is faster, more exciting and much funnier than Wilde's. Orton set out to write a play as good as *The Importance of Being Earnest*. He ended up writing one that is considerably better.

Chapter Seven
Know thyself - Be thyself

How will Orton be remembered?

A play as funny and as cleverly plotted as *What the Butler Saw* will certainly survive. Audiences will continue to be dazzled by the frenzied action and brilliant wordplay long after the content has lost its power to shock. A play like *Entertaining Mr Sloane* which relies more on outrage for its effect has a shorter shelf-life. Something still more outrageous will always supersede it. The simmering dialogue between Ed and Sloane shocked audiences in the sixties but pales in comparison with the full-frontal male nudity and homosexual groping of Kevin Elyot's *My Night With Reg* (1994.)

Will Orton's life always be more famous than his works? Will the enduring image of him be that of a man prowling London lavatories in search of rough trade? It would be a pity if it were as he spent considerably more time at the typewriter developing his talent. It is more fruitful to consider the life and the works in tandem. The philosophy that can be drawn from both his life and his works is that a person should reject conventional morality and follow his own nature. This is the lifestyle he practised. It was not in his nature to be heterosexual or monogamous. He had to hide his homosexuality from the press and the public to avoid harassment but he did not attempt to hide it from himself. Many men of his time, on realizing they had homosexual leanings, would have styled themselves 'confirmed bachelors' and avoided sex altogether. Others would have lived a lie and followed the conventional path of marriage. Orton flouted both legality and the widely-held morality of his day by being actively homosexual. He also did not hide the fact that his sexual interests were not confined to just one man: he was honest with himself and with Halliwell. He did not deceive Halliwell with stories about working late. Rather, he recorded all his infidelities in the diary which he knew Halliwell read. He picked up young boys while on holiday with

Halliwell and encouraged Halliwell to do the same. If he had been more discreet, he might have lived a lot longer. But he saw no reason to be discreet with Halliwell: he was not doing anything that made him feel ashamed. Indeed, he proselytized with messianic fervour about promiscuous homosexuality to such friends as Kenneth Williams. Orton's diaries reveal a man who was prepared to be honest about who he was, a man who defiantly refused to allow society to curb his nature. He followed his inclinitions, even into areas that were illegal or supposedly immoral.

In the plays, he is more concerned with showing the problems a person encounters by not following his heart. Orton rarely shows characters who reach happiness and fulfilment through being true to their natures. He rather shows characters whose problems stem from their attempts to conceal their natures behind conventional decency and respectability. The source of Dr Prentice's problems is not so much his attempt to seduce Geraldine as his attempt to conceal the seduction from his wife. If he had told Mrs Prentice: 'You've caught me trying to seduce my secretary - let's discuss it and come to some arrangement about an open marriage,' he would have avoided the accusations of being a homosexual transvestite murderer. He is plunged into chaos by trying to hide his natural lechery behind his image as a respectable member of the medical profession.

It is only in *Loot* that his philosophy is presented positively. Hal, Dennis and Fay do not hide behind conventional morality. Their natures dictate that they steal and murder to achieve their ends. They have no interest in the established taboos concerning a corpse and a coffin. They are true to their own natures. Orton rewards their honesty by allowing them to finish the play with a large amount of money and no prospect of prison. When they do find themselves in trouble during the play, it is usually because Hal has been making his one concession to conventional morality by always telling the truth - a form of honesty that Orton did not value highly. Even Truscott is honest about his nature. He has no illusions of himself as a man of justice. He is corrupt and he knows it. He scornfully dismisses McLeavy's faith in the police as upholders of the law and protectors of the innocent. He too is allowed to end up on top. He has made an arrest and has his own share of the loot. Only McLeavy fails to be true to his own nature. He hides his ambivalent feelings about his wife's death behind an obsession that all the traditional trappings of a funeral must be in place. Orton punishes his hypocrisy by making him the play's punchbag. He is the one who is injured in the accident at the funeral. He is the one who takes the blame for the robbery. He is the one who is arrested and condemned to a mysterious death in a police cell.

Orton believed that chaos was the natural result of concealing one's true nature. In *Loot*, he shows that success comes from being oneself. His experience of writing the play and of its production in London also demonstrated this. *Loot* was his most successful play. It was also the play in which he stopped trying to be Ronald Firbank or Harold Pinter and started to be himself. By living life on his own terms, he became successful and happy. However, 'be yourself and reject convention' is not a complete philosophy of life. Rejection of convention is not something to be done without thought. Some conventions are in place for sound utilitarian reasons. The convention of monogamy – or, perhaps, the convention of pretending to be monogamous – has survived because promiscuity has a marked tendency to hurt people. One's own nature often needs to be tempered in deference to other people. Relationships are all about compromise and Orton refused to compromise. To do so would be to stifle his nature, to do the very thing he despised. He would not give Halliwell the monogamous relationship that Halliwell craved. He would not even give Halliwell the comfort of pretended monogamy. He did not see, or did not care about, the effect his actions were having on Halliwell. He followed his own nature, but followed it blindly. It cost him his life.

It could be argued that he could not have written the works if he had not lived the life – that the plays were born out of the lifestyle. This is certainly the view that Orton himself took. In his autobiography, Kenneth Williams recalls a conversation with Orton and Halliwell:

> 'Sexual promiscuity,' he [Orton] said, now provided him
> with material for his writing; 'I need to be a fly on the wall.'
> But Kenneth Halliwell disagreed: 'It's all right letting off
> steam on holiday but a home life should have the stability
> of a loyal relationship.' (*Just Williams*)

If what Orton said was true, then his life story starts to look like tragedy: the very qualities that allowed him to succeed led inexorably to his downfall. But was it true? As a justification for infidelity, it is, at first sight at least, rather less convincing than the traditional 'my wife doesn't understand me.' So did the lifestyle genuinely feed the writing?

As a drug-taking, promiscuous homosexual from a working-class background, he had excellent credentials to become the darling of the London theatrical scene but would never have been accepted in strait-laced, middle-class society. This was the society that he satirized. The objects of his fun were solidly middle-class – businessmen, the police, churchmen, doctors. Being outside this society gave him a standpoint from which to observe it. He was neither an actual nor an aspiring member of it so had no protective desire to show it in a good light. What contact he did have with the middle classes only confirmed his opinion of them. He encountered many a respectable man who spent half an hour in a lavatory or a week in Morocco indulging his homosexual passions before returning home to his wife and children. Orton looked in on middle-class life and saw natural desires suppressed by conventional decency and only occasionally breaking out, shamefully and in secret.

However, he too wanted to straddle two lifestyles. He wanted the life of the lavatory-hopping free agent but he also wanted the relative stability of domestic life with Halliwell. It's not easy to explain Orton's peculiar brand of loyalty to Halliwell. He may have felt that he could not leave the man to whom he owed so much and on whom he still relied for the first reaction to his writing. His home with Halliwell may have provided a framework to his life that he needed in order to work. On the other hand, he may have felt that his leaving would push Halliwell that last little way into suicide. Possibly, he simply stayed with Halliwell out of convenience and did not believe that Halliwell was strong enough to hurt him. He may have underestimated Halliwell just as Sloane underestimates Kath. Orton, like Sloane, believed he could get away with anything.

The body of work left when he died is more rich in promise than in achievement. He wrote one excellent play and eight which are flawed if often entertaining. *Up Against It* has the potential to be an enjoyable film in the same mould as Lindsay Anderson's *O Lucky Man!* (1973) – the tale of a man's journey through a crazy and often hostile world.

The main interest of his diaries lies in the insight they offer into the early months of the golden age of British homosexuality. The diaries cover the period from December 1966 to August 1967. On 27 July 1967, sex in private between two men over twenty-one was made legal. Even before that, more and more gay men were accepting their sexuality. The move from the lavatories to the bars was beginning. A gay scene in London was starting to emerge. While there is guilt and covert sex in *The Orton Diaries*, they predominantly show gay men enjoying themselves - increasingly free nòt only from the law but also from shame and, as yet, blessedly free from AIDS.

His novels were unpublishable when they were written and would be unpublishable still if they did not have a famous name on the cover. They are interesting only as offering the first glimpses of his talent.

Orton had a great flair for producing epigrams, whose elegance was often hilariously at odds with the scurrilous subject matter. However, his message to the world, if he had such a thing, was nothing more profound than 'be yourself and reject conventional morality' – an incomplete, and not even very original, philosophy. It is impossible to know how this philosophy would have developed and matured over time. He was murdered just as he had found his voice. The play he was planning as the follow-up to *What the Butler Saw* was to have been very different. He said of it:

I've written the first draft of a third play [*What the Butler Saw*] which will be a conventional form, but the ideas I've got for a fourth play won't be conventional form at all. So you see I'm not even committed to the conventional theatre. But I think one should prove that one can do it, like Picasso proved he could paint perfectly recognizable people in his early period and then he went on to do much more experimental things.

Picasso would have been a minor figure in the history of art if he had died having painted nothing except his early classical and post-impressionist works. Orton's words suggest that he suffered an equivalent fate. What he did write was merely paving the way for the more innovative work that was to follow. With his talent, the experiments in dramatic form that he was planning could have established him as a major playwright.

However, a writer must be judged on what he wrote, not on what he might have written. Orton is an interesting, but limited, figure. Those who admire his skill with words can only wonder what he would have achieved if he'd had more time.

Further reading

One book that anyone interested in Orton must read is John Lahr's biography, *Prick Up Your Ears*. Exhaustively researched and lucidly written, it provides an excellent insight into the man and his works. Lahr has also written incisive introductions to *Orton - The Complete Plays* and *The Orton Diaries*. C.W.E. Bigsby's *Joe Orton* is an intelligent study of the plays but often gets bogged down in the jargon of literary criticism. Apart from these books, Orton is not extensively covered in the literature about twentieth century drama. The reader is largely left to read *The Complete Plays* and *The Orton Diaries* and to make up his own mind.

Index

GREENWICH EXCHANGE BOOKS

STUDENT GUIDES

Greenwich Exchange Student Guides are critical studies of major or contemporary serious writers in English and selected European languages. The series is for the Student, the Teacher and the 'common reader' and are ideal resources for libraries. The *Times Educational Supplement (TES)* praised these books saying "The style of these guides has a pressure of meaning behind it. Students should learn from that... If art is about selection, perception and taste, then this is it."

(ISBN prefix 1-871551- applies)
The series includes:
W. H. Auden by Stephen Wade (-36-6)
William Blake by Peter Davies (-27-7)
The Brontës by Peter Davies (-24-2)
Joseph Conrad by Martin Seymour-Smith (-18-8)
William Cowper by Michael Thorn (-25-0)
Charles Dickens by Robert Giddings (-26-9)
John Donne by Sean Haldane (-23-4)
Thomas Hardy by Sean Haldane (-35-1)
Seamus Heaney by Warren Hope (-37-8)
Philip Larkin by Warren Hope (-35-8)
Tobias Smollett by Robert Giddings (-21-8)
Alfred Lord Tennyson by Michael Thorn (-20-X)
Wordsworth by Andrew Keanie (57-9)

OTHER GREENWICH EXCHANGE BOOKS

All paperbacks unless otherwise stated.

LITERATURE & BIOGRAPHY

Shakespeare's Non-Dramatic Poetry *by Martin Seymour-Smith*
In this study, completed shortly before his death in 1998, Martin Seymour-Smith sheds fresh light on two very different groups of Shakespeare's non-dramatic poems: the early and conventional *Venus and Adonis* and *The Rape of Lucrece*, and the highly personal *Sonnets*. He explains the genesis of the first two in the genre of Ovidian narrative poetry in which a young Elizabethan man of letters was expected to excel, and which was highly popular. In the *Sonnets* (his 1963 old-spelling edition of which is being reissued by Greenwich Exchange) he traces the mental journey of a man going through an acute psychological crisis as he faces up to the truth about his own unconventional sexuality.
It is a study which confronts those "disagreeables" in the *Sonnets* which most critics have ignored.
ISBN 1-871551-22-6; A5 size; 90pp

The Author, the Book & the Reader *by Robert Giddings*
This collection of Essays analyses the effects of changing technology and the attendant commercial pressures on literary styles and subject matter. Authors covered include Dickens; Smollett; Mark Twain; Dr Johnson; John Le Carré.
ISBN 1-871551-01-0; A5 size; 220pp; illus.

In Pursuit of Lewis Carroll *by Raphael Shaberman*
Sherlock Holmes and the author uncover new evidence in their investigations into the mysterious life and writing of Lewis Carroll. They examine published works by Carroll that have been overlooked by previous commentators. A newly discovered poem, almost certainly by Carroll, is published here. Amongst many aspects of Carroll's highly complex personality, this book explores his relationship with his parents, numerous child friends, and the formidable Mrs Liddell, mother of the immortal Alice.
ISBN 1-871551-13-7; 70% A4 size; 130pp; illus.

Norman Cameron *by Warren Hope*
Cameron's poetry was admired by Auden; celebrated by Dylan Thomas; valued by Robert Graves. He was described by Martin Seymour-Smith as one of "... the most rewarding and pure poets of his generation..." and is at last given a full length biography. This eminently sociable man, who had periods of darkness and despair, wrote little poetry by comparison with others of his time, but always of a high and consistent quality - imaginative and profound.
ISBN 1-871551-05-6; A5 size; 250pp; illus.

Liar! Liar!': Jack Kerouac–Novelist *by R. J. Ellis*
The fullest study of Jack Kerouac's fiction to date. It is the first book to devote an individual chapter to each and every one of his novels. *On the Road, Visions of Cody* and *The Subterraneans*, Kerouac's central masterpieces, are reread in-depth, in a new and exciting way. The books Kerouac himself saw as major elements of his sponta-neous 'bop' odyssey, *Visions of Gerard* and *Doctor Sax*, are also strikingly reinter-preted, as are other, daringly innovative writings, like 'The Railroad Earth' and his 'try at a spontaneous *Finnegans Wake'*, *Old Angel Midnight*. Undeservedly ne-glected writings, such as *Tristessa* and *Big Sur*, are also analysed, alongside better known novels like *Dharma Bums* and *Desolation Angels*.
Liar! Liar! takes its title for the words of *Tristessa's* narrator, Jack, referring to himself. He also warns us 'I guess, I'm a liar, watch out!'. R. J. Ellis' study provoca-tively proposes that we need to take this warning seriously and, rather than reading Kerouac's novels simply as fictional versions of his life, focus just as much on the way the novels stand as variations on a series of ambiguously-represented themes: explorations of class, sexual identity, the French-Canadian Catholic confessional, and addiction in its hydra-headed modern forms. Ellis shows how Kerouac's deep anxieties in each of these arenas makes him an incisive commentator on his uncertain times and a bitingly honest self-critic, constantly attacking his narrators' 'vanities'.
R. J. Ellis is Professor of English and American Studies at the Nottingham Trent

University. His commentaries on Beat writing have been frequently published, and his most recent book, a full modern edition of Harriet Wilson's *Our Nig*, the first ever novel by an African American woman, has been widely acclaimed.
ISBN 1-871551-53-6; A5 size; 300pp

PHILOSOPHY

Marx: Justice and Dialectic *by James Daly*
Department of Scholastic Philosophy, Queen's University, Belfast.
James Daly shows the humane basis of Marx's thinking, rather than the imposed "economic materialistic" views of many modem commentators. In particular he refutes the notion that for Marx, justice relates simply to the state of development of society at a particular time. Marx's views about justice and human relationships belong to the continuing traditions of moral thought in Europe.
ISBN 1-871551-28-5; A5 size; 180 pp

Questions of Platonism *by Ian Leask*
In a daring challenge to contemporary orthodoxy, Ian Leask subverts both Hegel and Heidegger by arguing for a radical re-evaluation of Platonism. Thus, while he traces a profoundly Platonic continuity between ancient Athens and 19th century Germany, the nature of this Platonism, he suggests, is neither 'totalizing' nor Hegelian but, instead, open-ended 'incomplete' and oriented towards a divine goal beyond *logos* or any metaphysical structure. Such a re-evaluation exposes the deep anti-Platonism of Hegel's absolutizing of volitional subjectivity; it also confirms Schelling as true modern heir to the 'constitutive incompletion' of Plato and Plotinus.By providing a more nuanced approach - refusing to accept either Hegel's self-serving account of 'Platonism' or the (equally totalizing) post-Heideggerian inversion of this narrative – Leask demonstrates the continued relevance of a genuine, 'finite' Platonic quest. Ian Leask teaches in the Department of Scholastic Philosophy at the Queen's University of Belfast.
ISBN 1-871551-32-3; A5 size; 154pp

The Philosophy of Whitehead *by T. E. Burke*
Department of Philosophy, University of Reading
Dr Burke explores the main achievements of this philosopher, better known in the US than Britain. Whitehead, often remembered as Russell's tutor and collaborator on *Principia Mathematica,* was one of the few who had a grasp of relativity and its possible implications. His philosophical writings reflect his profound knowledge of mathematics and science. He was responsible for initiating process theology.
ISBN 1-871551-29-3; A5 size; 106pp

POETRY

Lines from the Stone Age *by Sean Haldane*
Reviewing Sean Haldane's 1992 volume *Desire in Belfast* Robert Nye wrote in The *Times* that "Haldane can be sure of his place among the English poets." The facts

that his early volumes appeared in Canada and that he has earned his living by other means than literature have meant that this place is not yet a conspicuous one, although his poems have always had their circle of readers. The 60 previously unpublished poems of *Lines from the Stone Age* – 'lines of longing, terror, pride, lust and pain' – may widen this circle.

ISBN 1-871551-39-0; A5 size; 58pp

Wilderness *by Martin Seymour-Smith*
This is Seymour-Smith's first publication of his poetry for more than 20 years. This collection of 36 poems is a fearless account of an inner life of love, frustration, guilt, laughter and the celebration of others. Best known to the general public as the author of the controversial and best selling *Hardy* (1994).

ISBN 1-871551-08-0; A5 size; 64pp

Baudelaire: Les Fleurs du Mal in English Verse *translated by F. W. Leakey*
Selected poems from *Les Fleurs du Mal* are translated with parallel French texts, are designed to be read with pleasure by readers who have no French, as well as those practised in the French language.

F. W. Leakey is Emeritus Professor of French in the University of London. As a scholar, critic and teacher he has specialised in the work of Baudelaire for 50 years. He has published a number of books on Baudelaire.

ISBN 1-871551-10-2; A5 size; 140pp

FICTION

The Case of the Scarlet Woman - Sherlock Holmes and the Occult
by Watkin Jones
A haunted house, a mysterious kidnapping and a poet's demonic visions are just the beginnings of three connected cases that lead Sherlock Holmes into confrontation with the infamous black magician Aleister Crowley and, more sinisterly, his scorned Scarlet Woman.

The fact that Dr Watson did not publish details of these investigations is perhaps testament to the unspoken fear he and Homes harboured for the supernatural. *The Case of the Scarlet Woman* convinced them both that some things cannot be explained by cold logic.

ISBN 1-871551-14-5; A5 size; 130pp

THEATRE

Music Hall Warriors: A history of the Variety Artistes Federation
by Peter Honri
This is an unique and fascinating history of how vaudeville artistes formed the first effective actor's trade union in 1906 and then battled with the powerful owners of music halls to obtain fairer contracts. The story continues with the VAF dealing with performing rights, radio, and the advent of television. Peter Honri is the fourth generation of a vaudeville family. The book has a foreword by the Right Honourable

John Major MP when he was Prime Minister – his father was a founder member of the VAF.
ISBN 1-871551-06-4; A4 size; 140pp; illus.

MISCELLANEOUS

Musical Offering *by Yolanthe Leigh*
In a series of vivid sketches, anecdotes and reflections, Yolanthe Leigh tells the story of her growing up in the Poland of the nineteen thirties and the second world war. These are poignant episodes of a child's first encounters with both the enchantments and the cruelties of the world; and from a later time, stark memories of the brutality of the Nazi invasion, and the hardships of student life in Warsaw under the Occupation. But most of all this is a record of inward development; passages of remarkable intensity and simplicity describe the girl's response to religion, to music, and to her discovery of philosophy.
The outcome is something unique, a book that eludes classification. In its own distinctive fashion, it creates a memorable picture of a highly perceptive and sensitive individual, set against a background of national tragedy.
ISBN 1-871551-46-3; A5 size 61pp